S0-CRW-456

5

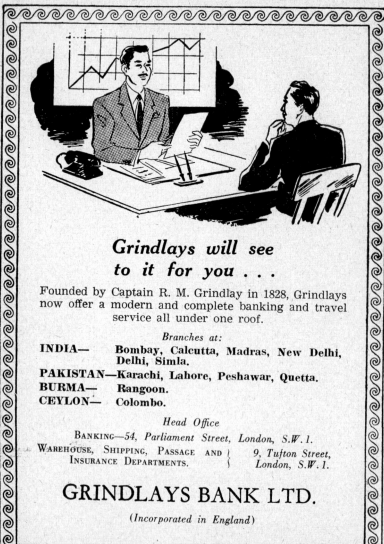

Travel in Luxury & Comfort...

... to see India's places of historical interest and beautiful natural scenery.

B.B.&C.I AND G.I.P
RAILWAYS
OFFER YOU

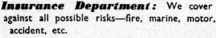

SEE KULU

THE VALLEY OF THE GODS

———

A S lovely as Kashmir, the Kulu Valley brings you face to face with the snow-capped peaks of the great Himalayas. Considered the last word in scenic beauty, Kulu unquestionably demands a visit from every visitor to India.

In the heart of this Valley stands the town of Manali with its exquisite pine groves and blooming apple orchards and several other alluring attractions besides a fascinating offer of sport to those who seek opportunities of Shikar and Fishing. Manali is also the gateway to the famous Rohtang Pass where the Beas river takes its source and across which extends the beautiful valley of Lahoul.

Manali, 200 miles from Pathankot, is approached from Nagrota, terminus of the narrow gauge Kangra Valley Railway. No other Railway in India approaches the famous " Snowy Range " so closely as does this line, which at several points is less than 10 miles distant from peaks whose altitude exceeds 15,000 feet.

Issued by EASTERN PUNJAB RAILWAY

SOAPS BY

PIONEERS IN ASIA.
Swastik have now
in operation the
latest continuous
soap making plant
— the only one of
its type in Asia,
making better
soaps than ever!

SWASTIK

SWASTIK OIL MILLS LIMITED, BOMBAY

SHILPI   SOM

TRAVEL
BROADENS THE MIND

Temple of Adinath KHAJURAHO

ELLORA

AJANTA

Meet your neighbours on the other side of the globe—see how they live and where they live—it makes life worth while.

INDIA—the fabulous land of colourful grandeur has so much to offer the traveller. The beauty of the **Taj Mahal** at Agra, one of the seven Wonders of the World—THE AJANTA FRESCOES and the stone sculptures of the MEENAKSHI TEMPLE at Madura, the work of expert craftsmen of centuries ago—The Holy City of BENARES with its fifteen hundred temples and its famous BURNING GHATS—KASHMIR with its romantic lakes and scenery, and the added appeal of Winter Sports—BENGAL with an opportunity for the hunter to 'bag' a tiger. We could go on for hours, but we invite you to Come To India and see for yourselves.

Thūpārāma Dagaba COLUMBO

Kutab Minar DELHI

Trade-wings

TRAVEL SPECIALISTS

Head Office : **30, Rampart Row, FORT, BOMBAY**

are happy to plan and undertake in detail your **personal** private, business or conducted travel in India and **Ceylon** by Air, Sea, Rail or Road. Special Hunting **Parties,** Himalayan and Tibetan Expeditions and Sight-**Seeing** Tours arranged.

We invite you to save your time by using ours, **for we** consider **your pleasure is our worry.**

For further information please contact our **Foreign Representatives,** C I T at :

ELEPHANTA

ROME : Piazza Esedra, 68. Telefono 43941— Telegrammi : "Centraleit" Roma.

BRUSSELS : Rue du Progres. 2 (Gare du Nord) Telephone 177693 — Telegram : Italcit

GENEVA : Rue Bonivard, 6 Telephone 2-91-23 Telegram : Italcit.

PARIS (Ufficio) : Bld. des Capucines, 1 (Paris 2eme) Telephone Opera 4085-4086-4087 Telegram : Italcit 108.

LONDON S.W. 1 : Panton House, 25, Haymarket, Piccadilly circus—Telephone Whitehall 7101-2-3 Telegram : Italcit—London.

Taj Mahal. Agra

LONDON S.W. 1 : FRAMES' TOURS LTD., 1, Regent St. Telephone : Whitehall 1548. Telegrams : FRAMREGENT, PICCY,

Keep your eye on **AHI**
for ★ PERFECT CUISINE!
★ EFFICIENT SERVICE!!
★ GRAND ENTERTAINMENT!!!

AHI with their traditions of quiet, unruffled ways, strain every effort to make your days as happy as you can desire.

Reference

AHI HOTELS
○ ASSOCIATE HOTELS
▲ OTHER HOTELS

Associated Hotels of India Ltd
& Associates

THE HANDBOOK OF
INDIA

Issued
for the Ministry of Transport
by
THE PUBLICATIONS DIVISION
Ministry of Information and
Broadcasting, Government of
India.

MARCH
1 9 5 1

Printed at
Glasgow Printing Co., Ltd.
Kadamtala, Howrah.

CONTENTS

TO THE READER

The object of this Handbook is briefly to give the visitor information about important tourist centres in India. It also contains other useful information which a traveller may require. Every care has been taken to make the book as accurate and up to date as possible, but the publishers do not accept responsibility for any inadvertent inaccuracy of detail. It is, of course, impossible to give in a short compass more than brief sketches of a few places only. For further information and details, the tourist is advised to contact the Regional Tourist Officers of the Government of India or travel agents before undertaking a tour. The addresses of the Tourist Officers are given below:

1. REGIONAL TOURIST OFFICER,
   Victoria Terminus,
   Bombay 1.

2. REGIONAL TOURIST OFFICER,
   Esplanade Mansions,
   Govt. Place East,
   Calcutta.

3. REGIONAL TOURIST OFFICER,
   88, Queensway,
   New Delhi.

4. REGIONAL TOURIST OFFICER,
   18-A, Mount Road,
   Madras.

IN RAJASTHAN

THE LAND AND THE PEOPLE

India extends from the Himalayas in the north to Cape Comorin in the south and covers an area of 1,220,000 sq. miles, which is roughly two-thirds the size of Europe excluding Russia. India is a land of rivers and streams, mountains, plateaus and forests of every kind. The rivers Ganga and Yamuna and their many tributaries water its northern plains, the cradle of Aryan civilization in India. The mighty Brahmaputra flows through Assam in the north-east. The Narmada, the Tapti, the Mahanadi, the Godavari and the Krishna are some of the other great rivers which have sustained the people of India through the ages.

India's civilization is one of the world's oldest, dating back to the end of the third millennium or beginning of the fourth millennium B.C. When the Aryans first came to India about 1500 B.C. they found a highly developed urban civilization in the country which was much superior to their own. The cities were well-planned, with wide roads, sanitary drainage, baths, and granaries while the houses were built of burnt bricks. Writing and the techniques of working metals were known to the people. Out of the intermingling of the Aryan with the pre-Aryan culture of India developed the three great religions, namely, Vedic Hinduism, Buddhism and Jainism and their systems of philosophy. On the material side, the visible symbols of the country's achievement were the great temples, monasteries, sculptures and frescoes which still attract visitors from many lands.

Even in the earliest period, India had trade relations with far off countries such as Babylonia. Later, its market for raw materials and industrial products extended as far as Egypt and the Roman empire in the West and China in the East. Its culture spread to all neighbouring countries such as Central Asia, Afghanistan, Persia, Ceylon, Indonesia, Burma and China. Islam came to India through the Arab traders and invaders in the eighth century. The Muslim kings, in particular the Mughals, added to India's cultural heritage. In the seventeenth century the impact of the

23

West was felt and in its wake came modern science, technology and the present-day democratic institutions.

In population India is second only to China. Her 350 millions represent one-seventh of the human race. This population is a great racial mosaic. A variety of customs and costumes obtain in the country. The people are hard-working, thrifty and hospitable.

The Indian Republic comprises twenty-seven States which are democratically administered. Some of the units are larger than Great Britain or Italy. At the head of the Republic is the President. The executive authority vests in a Council of Ministers responsible to Parliament which under the new Constitution will consist of an Upper House and a Lower House. The Lower House or the House of the People will be elected on the basis of adult franchise. The States, save those administered directly by the Centre, have constitutional heads who are assisted by Councils of Ministers responsible to the local legislatures.

Hindi is the State language of India, but English is understood by all educated people, tourist guides and hotel staff. Many of the leading newspapers and journals are published in English and so are the railway and airline time tables.

Almost all the religions of the world are represented in the country. Hinduism is the predominant religion. It counts 240 million people among its adherents. Of the remaining population Muslims are more than 40 million and the most numerous. Christians, Sikhs, Buddhists, Parsis and Jews are among the other religious groups.

Spreading as she does for nearly 2,000 miles from the sub-tropics in the south to the freezing north, India has a varied climate. The weather changes seasonally, and from region to region. Generally the winter months (November-March) are pleasant throughout the country. In northern India, it is at times very cold and there are heavy snow-falls on the hills. In eastern India, however, the cold spell does not last long. In Bombay and the south, there is no cold weather as such, but hill resorts about 5,000 to 6,000 ft. above sea level offer cool and bracing climate. The summer (April-June) in India is generally hot. Even in the hottest summer, however, a visitor can go to cool health resorts in the hills for which India is so well known. Places such as Kashmir, the Kulu Valley, Simla, Mussoorie, Nainital, Darjeeling, Ooty, Kodaikanal are delightfully pleasant during the summer months. The temperature does not rise beyond 60 to 70 degree on an average. The country receives its annual rainfall from the monsoon which breaks in July and is active till the end of September. In short, all the year round, a visitor to India can find the type of climate he likes at one place or other.

All the important places in India are well connected by rail, road, and air. The country has her own standard time, the Indian Standard Time (I.S.T.), which is 5½ hours in advance of the G.M.T. The Indian Standard Time is the railway time throughout India.

WHAT INDIA OFFERS TO THE TOURIST

No region in the world is more colourful and picturesque than India. Its ancient monuments and buildings designed by master craftsmen of bygone days, its customs, festivals, religions, philosophy and art testify to one of the oldest and richest civilizations and are of absorbing interest. To the lover of nature, the botanist and the naturalist, India offers every charm in forest, mountain, valley, cultivated plain or desert waste.

For the sportsman, India furnishes sport such as few countries do : tiger, panther, bear, elephant, buffalo and bison in the forests, trout and mahseer in the rivers, the wily snipe and the strong-winged duck on the jheels, and the quick turning pig in the jungles and, of course, racing, polo, golf, cricket, tennis, sea-bathing and even winter sports. To the mountaineer, the Himalayas offer the highest mountains in the world, with their many famous peaks which have not yet been scaled.

The art collector and souvenir hunter will reap a good harvest in this country. India's arts and crafts have always been prized abroad. An instinctive feeling for beauty, infinite patience and the accumulated experience of centuries enable the Indian craftsman to produce goods of rare excellence and design. Kashmir is justly renowned for the exquisite patterns and colours of its hand-embroidered shawls. The brocades of Banaras and Murshidabad, the jewellery of Delhi and Jaipur, the ivories of Mysore and Travancore, the inlaid metalware of Moradabad and Hyderabad and the glass bangles of Firozabad are some of the infinite variety of Indian crafts which appeal to the eye and satisfy the aesthetic urge of the connoisseur and the layman alike.

HOW TO REACH INDIA

The traveller has the choice of many air and steamship lines for his journey. The air and steamship routes to India are as follows:

AIR ROUTES

Name of Company	Route
1. AIR INDIA INTERNATIONAL LTD., BOMBAY	London-Geneva-Rome-Cairo-Bombay Nairobi-Aden-Karachi-Bombay
2. AIR INDIA LTD., BOMBAY	Colombo-Tiruchirapalli-Madras-Bombay Karachi-Ahmadabad-Bombay
3. AIR CEYLON	Colombo-Jaffna-Madras Colombo-Jaffna-Tiruchirapalli Singapore-Colombo-Bombay-Karachi- Cairo-Rome-London
4. AIR FRANCE	Paris-Rome-Cairo-Bahrein-Karachi Delhi-Calcutta-Saigon
5. BRITISH OVERSEAS AIRWAYS CORPORATION	London-Rome-Cairo-Karachi-Calcutta- Singapore-Jakarta-Darwin-Sydney London-Rome-Cairo-Bahrein-Karachi- Delhi-Calcutta London-Rome-Cairo-Basra-Karachi- Calcutta-Rangoon-Bangkok- Hongkong-Tokyo London-Rome-Cairo-Bahrein-Bombay- Colombo-Singapore-Hongkong

Name of Company	Route
6. BRAATHENS	Oslo-Stavanger-Amsterdam-Geneva-Rome Athens-Cairo-Abadan-Karachi-Bombay-Calcutta-Bangkok-Hongkong
7. BHARAT AIRWAYS LTD.	Singapore-Bangkok-Calcutta
8. ETHIOPIAN AIR LINES INC.	Nairobi-Addis Ababa-Aden-Karachi-Delhi-Bombay
9. IRANIAN AIRWAYS CO.	Tehran-Esfahan-Yazd-Kerman-Zahedan-Karachi-Bombay
10. K. L. M.—ROYAL DUTCH AIRLINES	Amsterdam-Munich-Geneva-Rome-Cairo-Damascus-Baghdad-Basra-Dhahran-Karachi-Calcutta-Bangkok-Singapore-Jakarta
11. ORIENT AIRWAYS LTD.	Karachi-Delhi-Calcutta-Dacca Karachi-Lahore-Delhi-Dacca Dacca-Calcutta Rangoon-Chittagong-Calcutta Akyab-Chittagong-Calcutta
12. QANTAS EMPIRE AIRWAYS LTD.	Sydney-Darwin-Singapore-Calcutta-Karachi-Cairo-Rome-London Sydney-Darwin-Singapore-Colombo-Bombay—Karachi-Cairo-Rome-London
13. PAN AMERICAN WORLD AIRWAYS SYSTEM	New York-Boston-Gander-Shannon-London-Brussels-Munich-Istanbul-Beirut-Damascus-Basra-Karachi-Delhi-Calcutta-Bangkok-Hongkong Manila-Okinawa-Tokyo-Guam Island-Wake Island-Midway Island-Honolulu-Los Angels-San Francisco-Portland-Seattle
14. PHILLIPINE AIR-LINES	Manila-Calcutta-Karachi-Lydda-Rome-Madrid-London

27

Name of Company	Route
15. SCANDINAVIAN AIRLINES	*Stockholm-Copenhagen-Frankfurt-Zurich-Rome-Lydda-Karachi-Calcutta-Bangkok*
16. TRANS WORLD AIRLINE	*New York-Gander-Shannon-Paris-Zurich-Geneva-Rome-Athens-Cairo-Basra-Dhahran-Bombay*

STEAMSHIP ROUTES

Name of Company	Route
1. AMERICAN PRESIDENT LINE	*Monthly sailings between America and India by the round-the-world route*
2. ANCHOR LINE LTD.	*Monthly passenger service from Liverpool to Bombay via Port Said, Aden and Karachi*
3. BOMBAY STEAM NAVIGATION COMPANY	*Weekly sailings between Karachi and Bombay*
4. BRITISH INDIA STEAM NAVIGATION CO.	*Regular passenger service from Japan, China, Malaya and Rangoon to Calcutta; and East and South Africa, Persian Gulf ports and Pakistan to Bombay*
5. EAST ASIATIC LINES	*Sailings from Red Sea, Mediterranean and North Sea ports to Bombay, Madras and Calcutta*
6. EVERETT STAR LINE	*Monthly service from Basra, Khorramshahr, Kuweit, Bahrein, Karachi to Bombay and from Kobe, Hongkong, Singapore, Penang, Colombo to Bombay*
7. INDIAN AFRICAN LINE	*Steamship service from East and South Africa to Madras and Calcutta*
8. INDO-CHINA LINE	*Steamship service from Japan, China, and Malaya to Calcutta*

Name of Company	Route
9. LLOYD TRIESTINO LINE	Monthly cargo-cum-passenger boat sailings between Italy and India
10. MOGUL LINE	Sailings between Red Sea ports and India
11. PENINSULAR & ORIENTAL STEAM NAVIGATION Co.	Regular passenger service between U.K., India, Australia and the Far East
12. SCINDIA STEAM NAVIGATION Co.	Regular passenger service between Europe and India

USEFUL HINTS

PASSPORTS AND VISAS

Every person entering India is required to be in possession of a valid passport issued by his Government. The visitor should also obtain a visa for India from the Indian representative or from the British representative if there is no Indian representative in his country. Commonwealth citizens are exempt from the visa requirement; persons of non-Indian origin domiciled in South Africa are, however, required to obtain entry permits.

REGISTRATION

The foreigner entering India is required to get himself registered at the port of arrival and also to obtain a "residential permit" specifying the period for which he is permitted to stay in India.

A foreigner who enters India as a "tourist" will be registered as such. Unlike other foreigners, tourists will not be required to report their movements. The period for which a "tourist" is normally allowed to stay in India is three months.

CUSTOMS

Bona fide baggage of passengers is allowed free. Bona fide baggage includes clothes, personal effects and reasonable quantities of household effects, provided the articles are imported for the personal use of the passenger or members of his|her family travelling with him|her and are not for sale or for the use of other persons.

For full details regarding Customs procedure enquiries may be addressed to the nearest Collector of Customs or to the Regional Tourist Officers.

CLEARANCE OF BAGGAGE

The tourist will find it convenient to entrust the clearing and forwarding of baggage to recognized travel agents. If porters are engaged, their badge numbers should be noted.

CURRENCY REGULATIONS

Tourists can bring with them any amount of currency notes and coins. In respect of the following, however, the amount is limited.

Bank of England notes	..	£ 5 per head
St. dollar „	..	$ 45 per head
Egyptian „	..	E. £ 20 per head
Australian „	..	A. £ 10 per head
Burma Notes		Nil
Indian notes from Burma	..	Rs. 100 per head
Govt. of India one rupee notes from Pakistan and Afghanistan		Nil
Indian coin from Pakistan and Afghanistan	..	Rs. 5 in value per head

Tourists have to make a declaration in the prescribed form to the Customs authorities and to get it countersigned by them. Currency in excess of the prescribed limits can be deposited with the Customs and receipt obtained. At the time of leaving India, the tourist can take back the money on production of the receipt.

It is unlawful to transact business except through an authorized dealer in foreign exchange.

The official rates of exchange are:

£ 1—Rs. 13.33
$ 1—Rs. 4.76

Buying and selling rates of the banks will, however, be a fraction less or more than the official rates.

INDIAN CURRENCY

The currency commonly in use consists of the Reserve Bank of India notes in denominations of Rs. 100, 10, 5, 2 and Re. 1 and coins. The official legal tender is the Indian rupee. The coins are:

> 1 pice
> ½ anna (two pice)
> 1 anna
> 2 annas
> 4 annas
> 8 annas
> 1 rupee

Based on the average rate of exchange, the rupee equivalents are:

Indian	British	American
1 pice	1 farthing	..
4 pice—1 anna	1 penny (approx.)	..
16 annas—1 rupee	1s. 6d.	21 cents
13 rupees 6 annas	£1 sterling	..
4 rupees 12 annas (approx.)	..	1 dollar

POSTAL INFORMATION

Normal working hours:

Week day	..	10 A.M. to 5 P.M.
Saturday	..	10 A.M. to 1 P.M.
Sunday	..	No work is transacted, but at certain important places letters are accepted on payment of late fee.

Mails are delivered throughout India on week days and Saturday, and in the big cities there are several deliveries every day. There is no delivery of mails on Sunday, but express delivery articles are delivered at certain places by telegraph offices.

Where facilities for air travel exist, letters and post-cards are carried by air without any surcharge. A small air mail fee at the rate of one anna per tola on packets and newspapers, and 10 annas per 20 tolas on parcels is charged for transmitting these articles by air.

Postage rate for the inland letter is 2 annas for the first tola (½ ounce approximately), and 1½ annas for the inland letter-card corresponding to the air letter for foreign countries. Air mail rates for letters to foreign countries are, among others, Rs. 1|8|- for the U.S.A.,

Canada and other countries in North and Central America, and 12 annas for countries in Europe, per half ounce. An air letter service is also available to all foreign countries the rates being 6 annas for most countries in Asia and for European countries, 8 annas for Australia, New Zealand and for African countries, 10 annas for the U.S.A., Canada and other countries in North and Central America, and 12 annas for South American countries.

Telegrams are accepted at principal telegraph offices and main post offices on all days of the week at all hours. For ordinary inland telegrams 12 annas are charged for the first 8 words and one anna for each additional word. The rates for express telegrams are twice those for ordinary telegrams.

CLOTHES

The cold weather lasts from November to March. In northern India it can be very cold and frosty, particularly at night, but the days are usually sunny and pleasant. In Bombay and Calcutta, the climate is milder, while the South is warm. To suit this variation of climate the tourist should have a careful selection of clothes. A supply of winter clothes and light summer wear is essential while a medium weight overcoat should be carried in the North where a sudden fall of temperature is usual after sunset. During the day a solar hat will be found useful.

Clothes can easily be made throughout India to suit all tastes. English suiting and shirting materials are available and tailoring is of a high standard. A warm suit, for instance, which would take 2 to 3 months to make in the U.K., and cost £30 to £40 can be had ready within a week in India and cost Rs. 250 to 350. A tourist can easily supplement his wardrobe in India at a reasonable cost without any difficulty.

TRAVELLING SERVANTS

Servants are not an absolute necessity, but a good servant is well worth the expense. He will be particularly useful during a railway journey. He will act both as interpreter and valet. Travelling servants are available from travel agencies.

CONVEYANCE

Taxicabs are available for hire in all principal cities. Taxi fares are reasonable, but vary from place to place. Generally they are between eight annas and one rupee per mile.

TOURIST AGENCIES

The following is a list of some of the tourist agencies :—

1. MESSRS. AMERICAN EXPRESS COMPANY. INC.,
   Navsari Building, 240, Hornby Road,
   Post Box No. 507, Bombay 1.

2. MESSRS. BALMER LAWRIE & CO., LTD.,
   21, Netaji Subhas Road, Calcutta 1.

3. MESSRS. BHARAT TRAVEL SERVICE, LTD.,
   Vanguard House, 11 & 12, Second Line Beach,
   Madras 1.

4. MESSRS. COX & KINGS (Agents) LTD.,
   Lloyds Bank Building, Hornby Road,
   Post Box No. 398, Bombay 1.

5. MESSRS. GOVAN AGENCIES LTD.,
   Post Box No. 10, Scindia House,
   Connaught Circus, New Delhi.

6. MESSRS. GRINDLAYS BANK LTD.,
   Post Box No. 93, Mint Road, Bombay 1.

7. MESSRS. INTERNATIONAL CARRIERS LTD.,
   32, Rampart Row, Bombay.

8. MESSRS. IYER & SON LTD.,
   Scindia House, Connaught Circus, New Delhi.

9. MESSRS. JEENA & CO.,
   10, Churchgate Street.
   Fort, Post Box No. 849, Bombay 1.

10. MESSRS. LEE & MUIRHEAD (India) LTD.,
    12, Rampart Row, Fort, Bombay.

11. MERCURY TRAVELS (India) LTD.,
    Post Box No. 8923, Calcutta.

12. MESSRS. ORIENT EXPRESS CO., LTD.,
    Marina Hotel, New Delhi.

13. Messrs. RAM MOHAN & CO., LTD.,
    National Insurance Buildings,
    362, Netaji Subhas Bose Road, Madras.

14. Messrs. THOMAS COOK & SON LTD.,
    Hornby Road, Bombay 1.

15. Messrs. TRAVEL AIDS,
    15, Barakhamba Road, New Delhi.

16. Messrs. TRADE WINGS,
    30, Rampart Row, Bombay.

17. Messrs. TULSIDAS KHIMJI,
    46, Churchgate Street, Fort, Bombay.

18. Messrs. VENSIMAL BASSARMAL & BROS.,
    New Silk Bazar, Kalbadevi Road,
    Post Box No. 2112, Bombay 2.

BOMBAY

A PICTORIAL TOUR

Part I

WESTERN INDIA

*Western India extends from the peninsula of Saurash-
tra in the north to the southern boundary of Bombay
State. The greater part of Western India is a narrow
fertile plain lying at the foot of the Western Ghats, whose
broken crags and strange-looking, precipitous, square-cut
peaks are an outstanding feature of the country. On the
summits of the rocky hills stand the ruins of the ancient
hill forts of the Marathas. Beyond the Ghats are plains—
great cotton-growing tracts, feeding the textile mills of
Bombay, Ahmadabad and Broach.*

BOMBAY

A beautiful harbour studded with hilly islands, and a
palm-fringed shore rising gradually to the peaks of mountain ranges, form a fine water-front for Bombay, the
"Gateway of India."

From the small straggling, unpretentious fishing
village of "Mumbai," it has grown to be one of the world's
greatest seaports. In 1534 the Sultan of Gujarat ceded it
to the Portuguese. The king of Portugal transferred it to
England in 1661, as part of the dowry of Catherine of
Braganza on the occasion of her marriage with Charles II.
A few years later, Charles leased Bombay to the East
India Company for the trifling sum of ten pounds a year.
At the time of transfer the place consisted of seven islands
separated at high tide by the sea which at low tide left a
wilderness of malarious mud flats. By steady reclamation
and improvement in drainage this pestilential swamp has
been transformed into a great city.

Besides being the chief import and export emporium
of India, Bombay is also a great industrial centre. A
cosmopolitan city it owes its prosperity to the industry and

enterprise of its population of three million. Throughout
the day a constant stream of people keeps flowing in and
out of its stream-lined transport, smart business premises,
palatial hotels and busy textile factories. In the evening
the centre of interest is the city's splendid promenade by
the sea, the Marine Drive, to which ladies elegantly dressed
in saris add colour and gaiety.

The Fort area is the chief commercial centre. Along
the rocky ridges and on the slopes of Cumballa and
Malabar hills are the charming homes of Bombay's well-to-
do residents, the famous Hanging Gardens and the Parsi
Tower of Silence. The summits of these hills offer a
superb view of the city, one that is almost magical at
night.

Besides the Prince of Wales Museum and Art
Gallery, the other places of interest are the "Gateway of
India" on the Apollo Bunder, the Mahalakshmi temple, the

BOMBAY—The Elephanta Cave

hot springs of Vajreshwari, the Crawford Market, the Victoria Gardens, the Zoo, and the Elephanta Caves.

Bombay's amenities include the Mahalakshmi race course, the finest in the East, the Brabourne Stadium, with a cricket ground, an up-to-date Lido, the Breach Candy Baths, with an excellently laid out open-air swimming pool.

About two miles from Santa Cruz station and opposite the aerodrome is Bombay's popular seaside resort, Juhu. With a beautiful stretch of palm-fringed sandy beach, it is a lovely bathing place which attracts holiday makers from Bombay every week-end.

Some six miles south-east of Bombay, on a small island decked with tropical vegetation, are the famous cave temples of Elephanta dating back to the eighth century. Five in all, they contain huge carved deities and panels in relief. The most striking of the images is the Trimurti, a 19 ft. high, three-headed bust hewn from a single rock representing the triple aspect of Divinity.

LONAVLA

About eighty miles from Bombay is Lonavla, a famous camping resort with beautiful lakes and an ideal spot for picnicking during the hot season. The Buddhist caves at Karle and Bhaja are on the motor road from Lonavla. They date back to the pre-Christian era. The main shrine at Karle is carved out of a solid rock and is famous for its architecture.

POONA

Poona is 119 miles from Bombay. The distance is covered in about three hours by the "Deccan Queen," one of India's fastest trains. About 1,850 ft. above sea level, Poona has a bracing climate. It was the capital of the Marathas at the time of the Peshwas and is now of considerable educational and military importance. It has many old palaces and parks and one of the best race courses in India.

SURAT

Surat, on the river Tapti, is 163 miles from Bombay. Under the Mughals, it was the "Gateway to Mecca" as well

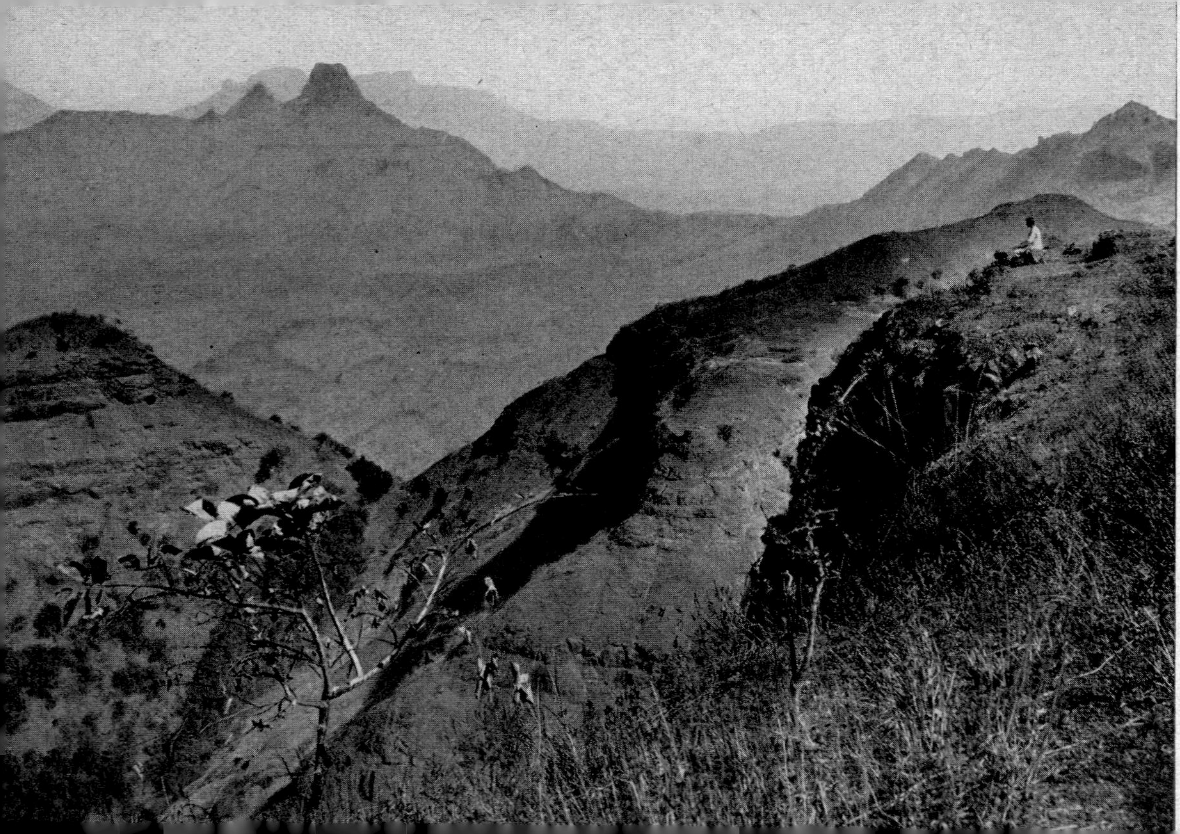

The Western
Ghats

as the chief port for the trade of Western India, and is still the home of a rich trading community.

Surat is surrounded by an old wall about five and a half miles in circuit with twelve gates. From the old castle on the river there is a good view of the city and of the Anglican Church founded and consecrated by Bishop Heber, while the remains of the old English and Portuguese factories look down upon the modern cotton mills.

BIJAPUR

Bijapur was once the splendid capital of a powerful sixteenth century Muslim State. "There is a combination of grandeur and grace about the architecture of Bijapur which is not approached elsewhere, and a beauty of ornamentation and execution nowhere exceeded."

Its finest building is the mausoleum of Sultan Muhammad Adil Shah, popularly known as the Gol

BIJAPUR—The Gol Gumbuz

Gumbuz. Built on a platform 600 ft. square, it has at each corner a tower seven storeys high. In the centre rises the enormous dome, 124 ft. in diameter, the second largest in the world. It is noted for its whispering gallery and multiple echoes. Among the other places of interest are the Citadel, the Sat Manzili, the tomb and mosque of Ibrahim Adil Shah and the Gagan Mahal. All that remains of the Gagan Mahal is the 90 ft. archway through which the last king of Bijapur was brought before his conqueror, Emperor Aurangzeb.

AHMADABAD

Ahmadabad stands on the river Sabarmati and is one of the industrial centres of Western India. Founded in 1411, it was "a goodly city as large as London" when Sir Thomas Roe visited India early in the seventeenth century.

Ahmadabad ranks high among the cities of India for its architectural remains. It has palaces, mosques and tombs, some of which are perfect specimens of Muslim architecture in Gujarat. The Jama Masjid, completed in 1424, is one of the most beautiful mosques in the East. Nearby are Teen Darwaza (The Three Gates) carved in sandstone. The best stone tracery work, however, is seen in the celebrated windows of Sidi Sayyid's mosque. The Rani Sipri mosque is another building of outstanding merit.

On the banks of the Sabarmati is the famous Ashram where Mahatma Gandhi lived and worked during the first half of his career in India.

BARODA

Baroda is now a part of the State of Bombay. Pleasantly situated on the banks of the river Vishwamitri, it is a modern city with broad avenues, palaces, parks and elegant buildings.

Outstanding among the places of interest in Baroda are the Lakshmi Vilas palace, built in Indo-Saracenic style, the Zoo, the Museum and the Picture Gallery of Indian and Western Art. The beautiful 125-acre public park on the banks of the river Vishwamitri, the Oriental Institute of Research and its valuable collection of ancient

BARODA—
Lakshmi
Vilas
Palace

PALITANA—Jain temples

Sanskrit manuscripts, the picturesque Sursagar tank, the well-laid out gardens at the Makarpura palace, the Nazar Bagh palace with its fine collection of jewellery, the show room of the Cottage Industries Institute, where Baroda's beautiful arts and crafts are exhibited, are some of the other places worth visiting.

PALITANA

Palitana is famous for its Holy Hill, Satrunjaya, the most sacred of the five hills of the Jains. From the summit of the hill, on which stand 863 Jain temples, there is a magnificent panorama. Some of the temples are probably of the eleventh century.

SAURASHTRA

The peninsular State of Saurashtra has many flourishing towns and ports which are connected by air services and are within easy reach of one another. The State has

JUNAGADH
—Jain
temples

large pearl fisheries along the coast and the Gir forest, the only remaining haunt of the Indian lion.

Among the leading cities of Saurashtra is Jamnagar, the home town of "Prince Ranji," the great cricketer. Pleasantly laid out, this modern town with its broad roads, picturesque markets, extensive gardens and open squares is known as the "Jewel of Kathiawar." It has a Radium Institute, an Aeronautical School and a Solarium, the only one of its kind in the East. Jamnagar is famous for its silk and gold embroidery.

In the ancient city of Junagadh is Uparkot, the stronghold of the former Hindu rulers of Junagadh. The

PORBANDAR—Mahatma Gandhi's birth place

fort has many relics of the past and its surroundings are honeycombed with Buddhist caves. To the east of the city is the temple-crowned Mount Girnar with its fine peaks. The temples are notable for their architecture and delicate carvings. On the way to Girnar is a rock with the edicts of Asoka (third century B.C.) and the inscription of the Saka Satrap Rudradaman (first century A.D.)

Porbandar is well known as the birth-place of Mahatma Gandhi. It is also an attractive summer resort, besides being a flourishing port which at one time carried on an extensive trade with Africa, Arabia and other countries.

Rajkot, the capital of Saurashtra, is also a picturesque city, a blend of the old and the new. It has a museum, a lovely park and two beautiful lakes.

Dwarka and Somnath are two other historical places dating back to the dim past. Plans are afoot to construct a new temple on the site of the ancient temple of Somnath, now in ruins.

MOUNT ABU

Mount Abu, reached by a good motor road from Abu Road railway station, is one of the prettiest hill stations in India. Near the Aravalli Range, it is situated on an isolated plateau nearly 4,500 ft. high, and has a lake of exquisite beauty. A place of pilgrimage for Jains, it has the celebrated Dilwara temples containing some of the finest specimens of Jain carving in India. Built of pure white marble, they have all the delicacy and richness of Indian art of the middle ages.

The forest sanctuary of Achaleswar is nearby.

GOA

Old Goa is now a city of ruins, except for the Arch-bishop's palace, the convents and the magnificent churches.

In 1510, the Portuguese captured the city of Goa and by 1565 it was the flourishing capital of an extensive Portuguese settlement. Descendants of some of the original Portuguese settlers still live in Goa and today about half the population of the settlement is Christian.

Old Goa was the scene of the labours of St. Francis Xavier and the holiest church in the town is the Bom Jesus, containing the body of the saint in a silver coffin.

ELLORA AND AJANTA

Near Aurangabad, a few hours' journey from Bombay, are some of the most remarkable monuments in India. The monuments at Ellora are of Buddhist, Hindu and Jain origin. Excavated in the scarp of a large rocky

AJANTA—A fresco

ELLORA—A rock-hewn temple

plateau, they are remarkable memorials of three great
faiths. The most marvellous of all is the stupendous rock-
cut Hindu temple of Kailasa, elaborately carved inside and
outside. Hewn entirely out of solid rock, with its massive
pillars and colonnades, intricate galleries, painted ceilings
and huge sculptures, Kailasa is one of the world's wonders.
It is estimated that the task of quarrying its 3,000,000 cubic
feet of rock must have taken at least a hundred years.

In a beautiful glade amidst superb scenery are the
caves of Ajanta consisting of twenty-four monasteries and
five temples some of which are 2000 years old. They are
excavated on a wall of almost perpendicular rock, 259 ft.
high, sweeping round in a hollow circle and extending a
third of a mile from east to west. Hewn out of rock, richly
sculptured and with walls, ceiling, and pillars, adorned
with fresco paintings, this cave picture gallery is unique
in the history of art. Nowhere else in the country is there
such an admirable combination of architecture, painting
and sculpture.

From Aurangabad the tourist can also visit the Bibi-
Ka-Maqbra, the mausoleum of Rabia Durani, erected by her

HYDERABAD—The Char Minar

husband, Aurangzeb, the tomb of Aurangzeb at Raoza and the fort of Daulatabad with a history of nearly a thousand years.

HYDERABAD

Hyderabad City, the capital of the State of the same name, has many splendid buildings—the Osmania University, the High Court, the State Library and the Falaknuma palace, considered to be one of the finest modern buildings in India. It has many fine public gardens, an interesting museum and a zoo, while nearby are the beautiful lakes, known as Osman Sagar and Himayat Sagar, the old fort of Golconda and the tombs of the Qutb Shahi kings. Eighty-two miles from Hyderabad in the pleasant little hill town of Bidar, on a plateau 2,330 ft. above sea level, are the ruins of beautiful buildings of the Bahmani kings.

The other places of archaeological interest in Hyderabad State are the Naganatha temple of Aundha in the Parbhani district, the great temple of Palampet in the Warangal district, the Mahadeva temple of Ittagi in the Raichur district, and the Vishnu temple of Dishpalli in the Nizamabad district. The Naganatha temple closely resembles the famous temple of Halebid in Mysore. Magnificent specimens of Muslim architecture are the Jama Masjid of Gulbarga, its entire area of 36,720 sq. ft. being roofed over (unlike any other mosque of India), the Chand Minar of Daulatabad, 210 ft. high and 70 ft. in circumference at the base, the Madrasah of Mahmud Gawan at Bidar, and the Char Minar of Hyderabad, built in 1549, a unique monument of its kind in India.

HAMPI

At Hampi, nine miles from Hoopet Junction on the M.S.M. Railway, lie the ruins of Vijayanagar, the ancient capital of the Vijayanagar Empire. The ruins, which have been described as "virtually a vast open-air museum of Hindu monuments in the Dravidian style of architecture," cover 9 sq. miles and are of extraordinary interest. The story of the rise and fall of this once "Forgotten Empire" is one of the fascinating romances of history.

HAMPI RUINS—Vithala temple

HAMPI RUINS—Elephant stables

PART II

CENTRAL INDIA

Central India has a tradition of romance and adventure, and is rich in artistic treasures. It comprises the States of Madhyabharat, Vindhya Pradesh, Madhya Pradesh (Central Provinces) and Bhopal. The paintings at Bagh, the exquisite carvings at Sanchi, the ruins of Mandu and the temples of Khajuraho testify to the cultural achievements of this region.

Running through Central India are the Vindhya Hills, with the rich wheat-growing country of the Narmada valley below its precipitous southern slopes, and the high Satpura Plateau, of forest-covered hills and deep water-cut ravines, declining into the Nagpur plain, where broad stretches of "deep" black cotton soil make it one of the most important cotton growing areas of India.

INDORE

Built by Rani Ahalya Bai (1765-95), the famous ruler of the House of Holkar, Indore stands on the banks of the rivers Saraswati and Khan, 1,830 ft. above sea level. It is about 440 miles from Bombay.

The old palace with its many-storeyed gateway faces the main square of the city. On the riverside are numerous Chhattris erected to the memory of the members of the Holkar family. In the Chhattri Bagh, an oblong enclosure with a battlemented wall, is the cenotaph of Malhar Rao Holkar I, richly ornamented with sculpture in low relief. Of modern buildings in the town are the King Edward Hall and the Lal Bagh palace on the river Saraswati amidst beautiful gardens.

MANDU

Fifty-five miles from Mhow is Mandu, the city of joy, on the crest of an off-shoot of the Vindhyas. It has a mild climate. Among its many ruins are the white marble tomb

of Hoshang Shah, a fit resting place for the great warrior and the Jama Masjid, the finest specimen of extant Afghan architecture; the Tower of Victory, formerly seven storeys high; the beautiful Jahaz Mahal with halls, swimming baths, turrets and cupolas; the Hindola Mahal, a well with subterranean retreats for the hot weather; and the famous Rup Mati pavilion built on a hill and looking down on the plain of Nimar, 1,200 ft. below.

BAGH

Bagh, 30 miles west of Mandu, has a number of large caves (fifth to seventh century A.D.) hewn out of rocks and adorned with fine frescoes which, even in their damaged condition, amply testify to the excellence of painting in those days.

UJJAIN

Ujjain is said to have been the seat of the viceroyalty of Asoka during his father's rule at Pataliputra (Patna). It is, however, best known as the capital of the legendary King Vikramaditya at whose court are said to have flourished the "nine jewels" of Hindu literature, of whom the poet Kalidas was the most renowned. Ujjain is 114 miles from Bhopal.

In Ujjain over the river Sipra is a picturesque palace known as the Kaliadah, a tribute to the engineering skill of ancient Indian architects. The Koshak Mahal, a noble four-storeyed edifice at Fatehabad, near Chanderi, and the Jama Masjid, the Shahzada-Ka-Roza and the Battisi Baodi at Chanderi are notable specimens of Pathan architecture. There are also the remains of an observatory erected by Jai Singh, Maharaja of Jaipur, during his governorship of Malwa.

BHOPAL

Half-hidden among mountains and resplendent with rich foliage, Bhopal, 521 miles from Bombay, lies in the heart of Malwa. It is hallowed by memories of the great Hindu King, Raja Bhoj. It was also once renowned as a prominent centre of Buddhist culture. An outstanding feature of Bhopal is its picturesque lake. The old wall which once encircled the city is still intact in many places. The Ahmadabad palace, situated on the crest of a high hill, commands a splendid view of the country for many miles around.

SANCHI

About twenty-five miles from Bhopal, on the rail route from Bombay to Delhi, is Sanchi, the site of the most extensive Buddhist remains extant in India. Its stupas are some of the oldest buildings in India. Most imposing is the great Stupa, a solid dome of stone, about 103 ft. in diameter and 42 ft. in height, built of sandstone. Round the base is a flagged pathway surrounded by a massive stone railing accessible through four gateways. The gateways and the railings are covered with bas-reliefs and inscriptions, written mostly in the script of the second and first centuries B.C. There is also a fragmentary pillar edict of Asoka. The most striking features of the Stupa are the gates which face the four cardinal points and measure 28 ft. 5 in. to the top of the third architrave, and are profusely carved with scenes from the Jataka stories. The carvings are vivid and true to nature.

SANCHI—Stupa—Eastern gateway

KHAJURAHO

SANCHI—Stupa

KHAJURAHO

About twenty-six miles from the ancient town of Mahoba lies Khajuraho renowned for its thirty magnificent temples. With the exception of three, they were all built between 950 and 1,050 A.D. and are unrivalled for profusion of ornate detail. In the Kandarya Mahadeva temple, the largest of the group, details of bewildering complexity are massed together to form a perfectly balanced unity. The Chaturbhuj temple stands on a high platform of masonry with smaller shrines in four corners. The Parswanath temple and the Ghantai are equally remarkable for their beautiful design, profusion of sculpture and graceful pillars.

GWALIOR

Rich in historic associations and architectural beauty, Gwalior abounds in objects of absorbing interest.

Standing on a steep isolated mass of sandstone, nearly two miles long, 2,700 ft. across at its widest and 300 ft. high, the magnificent Fort is one of the most impressive mediaeval strongholds of India. The ascent to the Fort is reminiscent of some fabled palaces in the Arabian Nights.

KHAJURAHO—
A temple carving

Passing through six massive gateways of elaborate
design, a broad road runs to the summit of the stronghold.
The most splendid of the palaces within the walls is
the Man Mandir, built by Raja Man Singh (1486-1516),
a specimen of the best Hindu architecture of its class.
It is described by Fergusson as "the most remarkable
and interesting example of Hindu palace of an early
age." The exterior with massive towers and latticed
battlements is covered with tiles of brilliant colour and
exquisite design, and the representation of elephants,
peacocks and other birds, in green, blue and gold mosaic,
lightens and enhances the contours. The Gujari Mahal,
also built by Raja Man Singh for his favourite queen, is
now an archaeological museum. Among the temples in the
Fort, two very interesting examples are those of the Sas-
bahu (the mother-in-law and daughter-in-law) which stand
on richly carved plinths, and date from the year 1093 A.D.
The Teli-ka-Mandir (the oilman's temple) is the loftiest of

KHAJU-
RAHO—
The
Kandarya
Mahadeva
temple

GWALIOR
—Man
Mandir
palace inside
the Fort

all the buildings in the Fort. Round the base of the Fort are enormous figures of Jain Tirthankaras (saints), one of them reaching a height of 57 ft.

Among the other places of interest in Gwalior are the Jai Vilas palace, a magnificent modern building of Italian design, which contains a splendid carpet reputed to be the largest and heaviest in the world, imposing marble cenotaphs of the Maharajas and the beautiful group of statuary erected to the memory of Her late Highness Maharani Sakhyaraja. In the old city at the foot of the Fort are the beautiful mosque and tomb of Ghaus Mohammed, a fine specimen of early Muslim architecture; and the mausoleum of Tan Sen, the famous musician whose name has become a legend. Musicians from all parts of India visit Gwalior to pay homage to his memory and singers chew leaves of the tamarind tree which grows near his grave to improve the quality of their voice.

JUBBULPORE

Jubbulpore, 616 miles from Bombay, is the second largest city in Madhya Pradesh (formerly C.P.). Thirteen miles away, at the bottom of the gorge of the river Narmada are the famous Marble Rocks. Near the entrance to the mile-long gorge is the Monkey's Leap. Nearby is the ancient temple of sixty-four Yoginis (female ascetics). About four miles to the west of Jubbulpore is an ancient fortress of the Gond Kings, the Madan Mahal, perched on the summit of a huge granite boulder.

SEVAGRAM

About seven miles from the Wardha railway station is Sevagram, where Mahatma Gandhi lived and worked for many years. In the Ashram (hermitage) founded by him live men and women pledged to a life of service. Some of Gandhiji's relics are kept in his hut which is visited by tourists.

Among the many creative activities which Gandhiji sponsored are basic education and village industries. The headquarters of the former, the Nai Talimi Sangh, which aims at promoting "learning by doing," are at Sevagram; and training in village industries is provided at Maganwadi in Wardha.

A Rajput

Part III

RAJASTHAN

Rajasthan covers an area of about 130,000 sq. miles, the greater part of which is a rocky and sandy desert interspersed with forests and fertile tracts. It is divided by the Aravalli range into two regions, eastern and western. Until recently it was known as Rajputana, and comprised, among others, the princely States of Udaipur, Jaipur, Jodhpur, Bikaner and Jaisalmer. The States of Rajputana have now been integrated into a single administrative unit called Rajasthan. Though administratively a separate unit, Ajmer-Merwara is part of Rajasthan, geographically, racially and historically.

Rajasthan, of all parts of India, perhaps, thrills one most, for here, among people of many races, live the Rajputs of ancient lineage and proud descent. Warlike in the best sense of the word, courteous and chivalrous, they have a stirring history of heroic struggle against overwhelming odds. In battle, they preferred death to dishonour. Nowhere in India will the tourist find so much that is traditional and picturesque as in Rajasthan, and though modern customs and costumes are encroaching on the old, the traditional warrior sense of the Rajput has led him to adopt the new so that his land presents a harmonious blend of the two.

JAIPUR

Jaipur, the capital of Rajasthan, is a magnificent sight. Surrounding it on all sides, except the south, are rugged hills, their summits crowned with forts. With embattled walls all round, the city was built early in the eighteenth century. It is so well laid out that it might well have been designed by a modern town planner. The Maharaja's palace stands in the centre of the city amidst charming

E

JAIPUR—
The Palace
of Winds

gardens. Houses with lattice windows line the streets. Their rose-pink paint lends colour to the scene and makes it almost magical at sunset.

Jaipur takes its name from the famous Maharaja Sawai Jai Singh, who founded the city in 1728. A keen astronomer, he built an observatory which still exists and equipped it with instruments of remarkable size. Also of interest are the Hawa Mahal, " the Palace of Winds," which has a splendid collection of old time weapons, carpets, ancient manuscripts and paintings, the Ram Niwas gardens, and the Albert Hall and Museum. Jaipur is noted for its craftsmen skilled in the art of cutting precious stones and is famed for its garnets. It is equally well known for brass work, lacquer work and the printing of muslins.

Amber, a deserted city, seven miles from Jaipur has an old palace overlooking the lake at the entrance to a rocky mountain gorge. Built in 1600 A.D. the palace ranks high architecturally. The " Hall of Victory " is so delicately ornamented with fine inlay work that it " glows with bright and tender colours." The fort of Jaigarh, crowning the summit of a peak 500 ft. high, is of amazing beauty and lonely grandeur.

UDAIPUR

Udaipur has been variously described at the " City of Sunrise " and the " Venice of the East." Here the visitor will find his dream of India come true, for the city combines real beauty with the picturesque associations of a great and glorious past. It stands in a valley, amid green hills, on the banks of a large lake of steel blue water, with little islands. On these rise from the water's edge marble palaces of pure white that glisten in the sunlight. Crowning the ridge, on which the city clusters along the lake's shore, is the palace of the Maharana. Within the palace is all the magnificence of the East—peacocks in mosaic on the walls, floors inlaid with tiles of rare design, and roof gardens affording thrilling views of the panorama below.

The island palaces, with their exquisite setting, rival the palace of the Maharana. The Jag Mandir palace, built in the first half of the seventeenth century, once gave shelter to Prince Khurram, (afterwards Emperor Shah Jahan) when he was in revolt against his father, Jahangir. The Jag Niwas palace, built a hundred years later, has delightful courts and gardens.

Udaipur has beautiful parks in which there are rose gardens and avenues of palms, and the vegetation is always fresh and green. At Odi Khas, the royal shooting lodge, the daily feeding of herds of wild boar at sundown is a unique sight.

Among the other places of interest in the city are the finely carved temple of Jagannath, built by Maharana Jagat

UDAIPUR—The palace

UDAIPUR—An island palace

UDAIPUR—State elephants

UDAIPUR—The Pichola Lake

Singh in the seventeenth century; eight sculptured arches between the Bari Pol and the Triple Gateway under which the Maharanas used to be weighed against gold which was then distributed to the poor; and the Sujangarh hill from which there is a splendid view of Udaipur.

Two miles from Udaipur, at the ancient village of Ahar, are the cenotaphs of the Maharanas, large and small, a wealth of white marble, interspersed with trees. Here, too, are *sati* stones—commemorating the courageous sacrifice of women who laid down their lives and passed away in fire at the death of their husbands. Fourteen miles from Udaipur, and linked by a motor road that runs through splendid scenery and a mountain pass, is Eklingji, a magnificent temple dedicated to Mahadeo. About 30 miles from Udaipur is Lake Jai Samand, one of the loveliest lakes in India.

Udaipur has a healthy climate. The heat is never excessive, for the town lies nearly 2,500 ft. above sea level. The winter months are delightful.

CHITORGARH

There is no place in Rajasthan with a history more romantic than that of Chitorgarh. It was here that Rajput

UDAIPUR

warriors repeatedly gave their lives, preferring death to dishonour and surrender. The city was sacked at least three times before it was finally abandoned and the capital moved to Udaipur. On the last occasion everything was destroyed except the Tower of Victory and parts of the old fort. The former was raised to commemorate Rajput victories over the invaders. It is a fine specimen of its class. The fort reposes on a rocky hill from the summit of which a view of the temples and ruined palaces can be had. Few can resist the urge to wander among these remains, every stone of which has behind it some tale of heroism or romance.

JODHPUR

Jodhpur stands on a range of sandstone hills surrounded by a strong wall, nearly six miles in length, with seven gates. Dominating the city is an eminence surmounted by a massive fortress. In olden days the fortress must have been well-nigh impregnable for the rocky base on which it is built is scarped on every side. A good metalled road winds up the neighbouring slopes to a massive gateway. This is the first of seven great barriers thrown across the zigzag ascent. Within the walls are royal palaces of old where one can see priceless jewels and a heterogeneous collection of arms. From the battlements there is a panoramic view of the city nestling round the fort. A view of the fort is to be had from the Gulab Sagar, a picturesque sheet of water within the city.

In contrast with its historical buildings, Jodhpur has many modern structures. Among the latter is an up-to-date airport, a stopping place for aircraft on the East-West route. Jodhpur is an important trading centre noted for its silk scarfs, lacquer and ivory industries.

In the nearby walled suburb of Mahamandir there is a fine temple, with a massive roof supported on a hundred pillars and a richly decorated interior. A few miles from Jodhpur, at Kailana and Balsamand, are picturesque lakes. The former is the headquarters of the Jodhpur Yacht Club, while the latter has extensive gardens and a small zoo. The well laid out Willingdon Zoological Gardens have a museum, a library, a sports stadium and a garden for women.

71

JAISALMER—The Fort

About five miles north of Jodhpur is Mandor, once the capital of Marwar. It was captured by the Rathor Rajput Chief, Rao Chonda, from the Parihar Rajputs in the year 1381, and served as the Rathor Capital until the foundation of Jodhpur. In Mandor are the cenotaphs of the former rulers of Jodhpur State, some of which are imposing, finely carved structures. Another object of interest is the Hall of Heroes, a gallery of sixteen colossal figures, hewn out of a single natural rock.

BIKANER

Bikaner, founded in 1488, is a desert city like Jodhpur. Built on an eminence and surrounded by a fine embattled wall, it is imposing in appearance.

Bikaner possesses many fine buildings. The fort, built between 1588 and 1593 by Raja Rai Singh, contains some old palaces, an interesting Sanskrit and Persian library and an armoury. Among several other interesting buildings in

CHITORGARH—The Tower of Victory

Bikaner are Jain monasteries, temples and mosques. Outside the city is a modern temple dedicated to Siva.

Bikaner is famed for its carpets.

AJMER

Ajmer, the capital of the small State of Ajmer-Merwara, was founded in the twelfth century by the Chauhamana ruler Ajayaraja. The city is dominated by the Taragarh

BIKANER—A richly carved building

fortress built by Akbar. Bishop Heber called it the "Gibraltar of India," and the name gives a clue to its stormy past. It changed hands many times.

Nearly 800 years ago, Ana built the splendid embankment by the lovely lake, the Ana Sagar, and some 500 years later Shah Jahan erected five marble pavilions of exceeding beauty. Akbar's fortress-palace, now a museum, and the Arhai-din-ka-Jhonpra are of interest, but outstanding in Ajmer is the Dargah Khawaja Sahib, the tomb of the famous Muslim saint, Muin-ud-din Chishti. The shrine has two mosques, one built by Akbar and the other by Shah Jahan.

Seven miles from Ajmer is the Pushkar lake sanctified by Hindu tradition.

BHARATPUR

The city of Bharatpur is known for its historic fort which withstood the British onslaught for a long time. About three miles from the city is a great marsh famous for its duck shooting. Twenty-three miles from Bharatpur and connected by a metalled road is 'Dig' with its splendid palaces which are noteworthy specimens of Indian architecture.

BIKANER—The Camel Corps

ALWAR

The town of Alwar is dominated by a fort which crowns a conical rock and is backed by a range of hills. At the foot of the fort is a beautiful tank. The palace has an interesting museum and an armoury. In the neighbouring forests, there is plenty of game, including panthers and tigers.

KOTAH

Kotah on the right bank of the Chambal river is a walled city. Among its many places of interests are the public gardens on the shore of a beautiful lake, a fine old palace, Umed Bhavan, the new palace, and the royal cenotaphs.

BUNDI

About twenty-eight miles west of Kotah is Bundi, situated in a narrow gorge in the hills. The wall round the city is pierced by magnificent gateways. The Bundi palace, by a lake, with islets on which there are temples, is a fine piece of architecture and one of the most beautiful buildings in Rajasthan. The Bundi jungles are noted for tiger shooting.

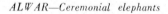

ALWAR—Ceremonial elephants

A Rajput warrior

BUNDI—
The Fort

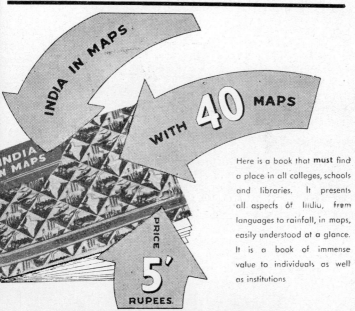

Something Different

A vacation in India
The land of sunshine and colour
Is something really different
Than what you have been accustomed to.
Sitting back home, you cannot imagine
The things that await you—
A bracing and agreeable climate
Good hotels and delicious food
And a friendly people.

★   ★   ★

The beautiful Taj Mahal - the Monument of Love
The historic city of Delhi built and rebuilt
Jaipur the Pink city where you will ride an Elephant
Benares the Holy city of Hindus
With its temples and burning ghats
And the vale of Kashmir—The playground of Asia
                          —The paradise on Earth
All are welcoming you.

★   ★   ★

We can plan an independent vacation for you
Or you can buy one of our package tours
To these places and many more
Which you can book in your home town in the United States
Through your Travel Agent and
Can depend on us for everything
From a sightseeing trip to a Tiger Hunt.

★   ★   ★

Now that your dollar goes much farther
Contact your Travel Agent who will plan a trip for you
Or write or call us at Hotel Marina, New Delhi
Phone 8156 Cable address Orexpresco
When our personalised organisation will be at your service.

ORIENT EXPRESS
Travel Service
HOTEL MARINA   NEW DELHI.

AUTHORISED REPRESENTATIVES OF AIRLINES, STEAMSHIPS & HOTELS.

Part IV

NORTHERN INDIA

Northern India is largely a land of great river-fed plains. In the north of this region are the Kangra and Kulu valleys in the Himalayas. West of the river Yamuna is the border State of the Punjab, the " sword arm" of India. On the river Yamuna is Delhi, the capital of India. East of the river are the fertile plains of Uttar Pradesh (United Provinces) where at Agra the world-famed Taj Mahal was built by Emperor Shah Jahan. On the river Ganga is the holy city of Banaras, probably the most ancient city in India and certainly one of the most picturesque.

AMRITSAR

A few miles within India's north-western border is Amritsar, known for its Golden Temple, the most sacred shrine of the Sikhs, and the tank called the Pool of Immortality. Ram Das, the fourth Sikh Guru, founded the city while excavating the holy tank; Guru Arjun Dev built the Temple. Ranjit Singh, the Sikh ruler, enriched the shrine and covered its dome with copper, overlaid with gold foil. The pool is enclosed by a wide, marble-paved

AMRITSAR—The Golden Temple

When you come to India

whether on business or pleasure, you are almost sure to travel a great deal. You will of course travel by air. You may now save your days for sight-seeing or business contacts and travel by night.

Fly in cosy comfort by India's premier night airmail —HIMALAYAN Night Service to and from Bombay, Nagpur, Delhi, Madras and Calcutta. It is safer, cheaper and most comfortable.

fly by
India's Premier Night Airmail
Himalayan Service

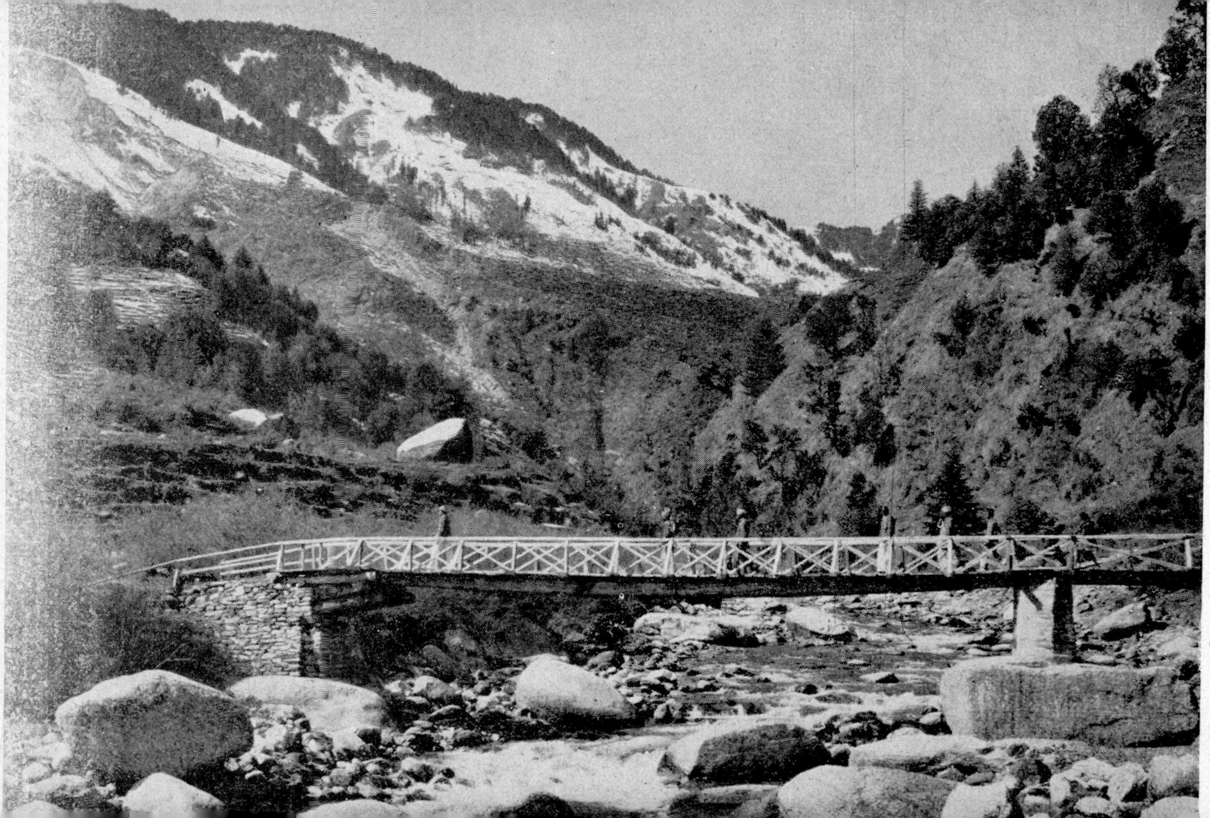

KULU VALLEY

quadrangle 204 ft. long with an archway over it. In the centre of the pool is the Temple, a square building with marble inlaid walls and dome-shaped roof, under which shaded by a silken canopy lies the Granth Sahib, the holy book of the Sikhs. In the Guru-ka-Bagh or the Garden of the Guru there is the Baba Atal Tower which contains interesting frescoes, depicting incidents from the life of Guru Nanak, the founder of Sikhism.

KULU AND KANGRA VALLEYS

Rivalling the vale of Kashmir in beauty, the Kulu and Kangra valleys lie at the foot of the Dhaula Dhar Range of the Himalayas. Green with apple orchards and strewn with ancient Rajput forts on the summits of immense crags, well-nigh impregnable in olden days, and with the majestic snow-capped mountains standing in bold relief against the sky-line, these valleys provide some of the best visual feasts in India.

Kangra, Jogindarnagar, Chamba, Dharmsala, Dalhousie and Kulu are some of the chief holiday resorts. Kangra lies on a hill 2,500 ft. high overlooking the Banganga stream. An ancient Rajput fort crowns a precipitous rock and dominates the surrounding valley. At Jogindarnagar, in beautiful setting, are the generators of a large hydro-electric station which utilizes the snow-fed waters of the river Uhl to generate electricity. Dalhousie a little beyond the northwestern corner of the Kangra valley, is 6,670 ft. high. From Dalhousie to Chamba the scenery is picturesque and the road passes through one of the most beautiful forests in the world. Baijnath, a sacred place for Hindus, has a temple, which is architecturally one of the best in northern India.

The Kulu and Kangra valleys are known for their orchards and tea plantations. Apples and pears are plentiful. In the winter the valleys abound in bears, leopards and other animals. The streams offer trout fishing.

SIMLA

Simla is a hill station, prettily perched on the spurs of the lower Himalayas at a height of 7,000 ft., its snow-capped peaks rising majestically against the horizon. This ideal health resort is reached from Kalka by a winding mountain

SIMLA—Government House

railway. As the railway ascends the hills, a delightful panorama unfolds itself. The journey from Kalka to Simla can also be done by car.

Simla has lovely scenery and fine walks to the woods of Mashobra and Mahasu with splendid views all round. Partridge and pheasant shooting in the neighbouring hills and racing at Annandale provide additional attractions. Hikers to Narkanda (39 miles from Simla) and Kotgarh (49 miles from Simla) can lodge in convenient rest houses on the way. Till recently Simla was the summer capital of India. It is now the capital of the Punjab and Himachal Pradesh.

DELHI

On the plains of Delhi, where now stands the splendid modern capital of India, cities have risen and decayed several times. Only their ruins mark the sites where they once stood. These Delhis of the past—the Red Fortress town of Anang Pal, the city built by Prithvi Raj, the capital of Kutb-ud-din, Siri, the city of Ala-ud-din, Tughlakabad, founded by the House of Tughlak, and Firozabad, the creation of Firoz Shah—together with Shahjahanabad, the city of Shah Jahan, of marble palaces and fine bazars,

DELHI—The Kutb Minar

of famous mosques and historic city walls, form a fitting historical background for New Delhi.

Shahjahanabad or Old Delhi, as it is now called, has many architectural masterpieces. The Red Fort dominates the city and stands as a mute symbol of Mughal glory. Inside it the visitor can see the relics of what was once the Imperial Palace of Shah Jahan. The two Audience Halls with their fine pillars and beautifully inlaid walls and ceilings are still a feast for the eye. On one of the walls, inside is inscribed a Persian couplet which says: "If a Paradise be on the face of the Earth, it is this—it is this, it is this." Other buildings within the Fort are the Rang Mahal, the Hamam, the Pearl Mosque and the Mumtaz Mahal which houses a museum containing relics of the Mughal Period.

From the Fort to the Fatehpuri mosque runs the Chandni Chowk, the centre for jewellers and gold and silversmiths, once renowned as the richest street in the world. A little to the south towers the famous mosque, the Jama Masjid, surely one of the noblest buildings in India. A magnificent flight of steps leads to its front court, which is 450 ft. sq. Paved with granite and inlaid with marble, it commands a splendid view of the city.

South and south-west of the city are the tomb of Humayun, a monument of rose coloured sandstone, inlaid with white marble; Tughlakabad, with its fine fort and the founder's tomb; and the Kutb Minar dating from the twelfth century, a tower of sandstone regarded as one of the

DELHI—The Jama Masjid

most perfect towers in the world. Nearby is the famous rust-proof Iron Pillar dating from the fourth century A.D.

New Delhi with its symmetrical buildings, broad tree-lined avenues and spacious parks is a planned city. It has a circular Parliament House and an imposing Central Secretariat, which stands at the approaches to the residence of the President of the Republic of India. The Lakshmi Narayan temple completed recently is also of interest.

DELHI—The Red Fort

DELHI—Red Ford—Floral decorations

On the right bank of the Yamuna is a hallowed spot —Raj Ghat, where Gandhiji was cremated after his martyrdom. The Samadhi, now raised into a platform surrounded by an enclosure, has become a national shrine. Every Friday, the day on which Mahatma Gandhi was cremated, prayers are held here. The Government of India plans to build a fitting memorial to the Mahatma on this spot.

AGRA

Agra, on the river Yamuna, was once the seat of royalty. Babar captured it in 1526 when the famous Kohinoor diamond formed part of his booty. Akbar made it his capital, built the Fort and ruled India from within its walls. It was Akbar's grandson, Shah Jahan, who built the world-renowned Taj Mahal, his immortal tribute to the memory of his beloved wife, Mumtaz Mahal. This beautiful mausoleum was built between 1630 and 1648, of pure white marble, on a vast marble terrace, with a great dome in the centre, surrounded by four smaller domes. At the angles of the terrace there are four slender minarets. Light passes through a double screen of pierced marble into the interior, where under the dome are the cenotaphs of the Emperor and his beloved wife. The interior decorations of inlay in semi-precious stones are remarkable for colour and design. Set in a spacious garden, of dark cypress trees, green turf and still waters, the pearly white dome and minarets seen by moonlight have a beauty which no words can express.

AGRA—Marble screen inside the Taj

THE TAJ

AGRA—Itimad-ud-Daulah's Tomb

AGRA—The Nagina Masjid inside the Fort

The Fort of Akbar, with walls seventy feet high, octagonal towers, and crenellated ramparts, one and a half miles in circuit, encloses a maze of courtyards, gateways, audience halls, mosques and private apartments. Here are the Jahangir Mahal, the fine palace built by Akbar, with admirable carvings in red sandstone; the Saman Burj, an octagonal tower beautifully inlaid with jasper, cornelian, and turquoise; and the exquisite Pearl Mosque, built by Shah Jahan, of pure white marble and unequalled for the beauty of its design.

On the opposite bank of the river is the tomb of Itimad-ud-Daulah, the father of Empress Nur Jahan. Of interest, too, is the Jama Masjid, built by Shah Jahan in the name of his daughter Jahanara, who shared his captivity when he was deposed by Aurangzeb.

At Sikandra, five miles from Agra, in a garden of great beauty, is the tomb of Akbar, strikingly impressive in its simple dignity.

FATEHPUR SIKRI

Twenty-six miles from Agra, on the spot where saint Salim Chishti foretold the birth of a son to Akbar, the great

FATEHPUR SIKRI—The Panch Mahal

FATEHPUR SIKRI—Shaikh Salim Chishti's tomb

FATEHPUR SIKRI—The Buland Darwaza

FATEHPUR SIKRI—
The Jama Masjid

FATEHPUR SIKRI—A marble pillar
in Shaikh Salim Chishti's tomb

Emperor built Fatehpur Sikri as a token of thanksgiving. Within fifty years the city was abandoned for lack of an adequate supply of water—and so it has remained a city of lonely grandeur.

The great mosque, containing Salim Chishti's tomb, surrounded by a screen of lattice work, and a canopy inlaid with mother of pearl, has the magnificent gateway, the Buland Darwaza, described by Fergusson as "noble beyond that of any portal attached to any mosque in India, perhaps in the whole world." In the Diwan-i-Khas Akbar once held discussions on religion with representatives of all religions. In the Pachisi court, laid out in red sandstone squares, he used to play chess with slave girls as pieces.

MATHURA

Situated on the banks of the Yamuna, Mathura, one of the oldest towns in India, is a city of temples. For miles the sky is pierced by their spires whilst the arches and marble galleries adjoining the ghats are of great elegance. In ancient times Mathura was an important centre of Hindu, Buddhist and Jain faiths. In the museum there is an interesting collection of sculptures, terracottas and inscriptions.

LUCKNOW

Lucknow, the capital of Uttar Pradesh (United Provinces), is a city of gardens. It stands on a bend of the winding river Gomti. Viewed from afar it presents a picture of gilded cupolas and pinnacles, turrets and minarets, interspersed with rich foliage. Outstanding among its buildings are the Great Imambara with a hall 162 ft. long and 54 ft. wide; the Husainabad Imambara, known as the "Palace of Lights;" the Rumi Darwaza; the grand Chhattar Manzil, once the residence of royal ladies and the Wingfield Park with its zoo.

Lucknow is famous for its gold and silver brocades, silver-ware, clay figurines and pottery.

KANPUR

Kanpur, a modern city, built by industrial enterprise, is an important manufacturing centre. Its busy factories turn out woollen and cotton textiles, brushes, and a large variety of leather goods.

ALLAHABAD

Allahabad, situated near the confluence of the rivers Ganga and Yamuna, is one of the main towns of Uttar Pradesh and an important centre of Hindu pilgrimage. Considerable interest attaches to the fort built by Akbar in 1575. Opposite the gateway inside the fort is Asoka's pillar, about 35 ft. high, with the famous edicts inscribed on it.

BANARAS

To the Hindus the 3,000-year old city of Banaras, sprawling along the left bank of the river Ganga, is the holiest city. With its array of shrines, temples and palaces rising in several tiers from the water's edge, Banaras is one of the most picturesque cities in the East. Jai Singh's

BANARAS—Vishwanath temple

Observatory, with its mural quadrants, giant masonry gnomon and quaint azimuth compass and the celebrated Golden temple are some of the many places of interest in the city.

BANARAS—River front

From time immemorial Banaras has been a centre of learning and the tradition is kept alive by the Hindu University.

Saris, brocades and brass-ware from Banaras are universally appreciated.

SARNATH

Hardly four miles north of Banaras is Sarnath where in the " Deer Park," Buddha delivered his first sermon after he became the " Enlightened One." The ruins of monas-

NAINITAL
—The Yacht
Club

teries built more than 1,500 years ago, the Dhamekh Stupa, the Dharmarajika Stupa, and the Main Shrine draw Buddhist pilgrims to Sarnath. The Main Shrine was originally the chief fane Mulagandhakuti about 200 ft. high and surmounted by a golden amalaka. The Mahabodhi Society of India have recently built a modern vihara known as the Mulagandhakuti vihara which, with its tower, is well worth a visit. Here stands the famous Asoka Pillar of polished sandstone whose lion capital was adopted by the new Republic of India as the state emblem. The museum at Sarnath, designed like a Buddhist monastery, contains many superb specimens of ancient art, including the capital of the Asoka Pillar.

NAINITAL

Picturesquely situated round the shores of a lovely lake, 6,350 ft. above sea level, Nainital is a Himalayan hill station of great beauty. Formerly the summer headquarters of the Government of Uttar Pradesh, it is a popular summer resort. On the lake, which is surrounded by green heights, there is excellent yachting and boating, swimming and fishing.

Not far from Nainital is Almora. From Almora some of the highest peaks of the western Himalayas can be seen against the horizon. The main attraction for hikers is the famous Pindari Glacier.

MUSSOORIE

At an altitude of 6,000 to 7,000 ft., cool and bracing in summer, Mussoorie is one of the most popular hill stations in northern India. Mussoorie is reached from Dehra Dun by car in about two hours.

KASHMIR — A trout stream

PART V

KASHMIR

A land of rivers and forests, of lakes and flower-spangled pastures, ringed round with stupendous snow-capped mountains, Kashmir is a tourists' paradise. It nestles in a valley which has been aptly described as an "emerald set in pearls." Its beauty was known to the Mughal Emperors, who laid out lovely pleasure gardens in Srinagar, the capital of the State. The Shalimar and the Nishat gardens rise in terraces, by the clear waters of the Dal Lake, against the background of steep, bare mountains. On the Dal, too, is the Nasim Bagh (the Garden of Breezes), with its stately chenar trees, and the Chashme Shahi, famous for its ice cold water.

Srinagar lies along the banks of the Jhelum, its waters crossed by seven bridges. A trip, down the river in a swiftly gliding *shikara*, gives a beautiful view of the city's quaint balconies, busy ghats, mosques and temples.

Gulmarg, thirty miles from Srinagar, is 8,700 ft. high, and is one of the finest pleasure resorts of Kashmir, popular for its skiing, trekking and other winter sports. Other health resorts are Khilenmarg, the botanist's paradise; Pahalgam, en route to the sacred Amarnath; Kokarnag, noted

KASHMIR—Lidder Valley

for the refreshing and curative waters of its springs; Achhabal, with a large spring; Lake Wular, one of the largest fresh water lakes in India; and Manasabal Lake, reputed for its lotus blossoms.

The impressive remains of temples, monasteries and mosques strewn all over Kashmir are also well worth a visit. The Buddhist monasteries in the eastern district of Ladakh; the Shankracharya temple, in the crest of a 1,000 ft. hill, overlooking the city of Srinagar; the famous temple of Martand, a mixture of Indian and classical Greek styles built on a bleak plateau; the mosque of Hazrat Bal overlooking the Dal Lake; the Jama Masjid, the biggest mosque in Kashmir built in 1404; and the Shah Hamadan, a rectangular mosque with beautiful carvings on doors and windows, are monuments of absorbing interest and symbols of a rich cultural heritage.

The colourful surroundings of Kashmir have imbued the Kashmiri craftsman with an instinctive feeling for beauty. His artistic genius finds expression in embroidery, woodwork, silver engraving, metal work, silk weaving, papier mâché work and carpets. *Pashmina* shawls are embroidered by hand in attractive colours and designs. In the nineteenth century Kashmir shawls were greatly prized in Europe and are in demand in India to this day. The State Exhibition in autumn, one of the main attractions of Srinagar, exhibits the arts and crafts of Kashmir, while the State Museum has specimens of Kashmir art, antiques and curios.

KASHMIR—A pastoral scene

KASHMIR

KASHMIR—
A girl from
Ladakh

KASHMIR—
A village
belle

KASHMIR—Verinag. the source of the Jhelum

Sport is among the many attractions of Kashmir. Hunters, anglers, lovers of skiing and trekking, all find their delight in the valley, and a charming holiday can be spent there in a houseboat.

SRINAGAR—The third bridge

KASHMIR—
Winter Sport,
Gulmarg

KASHMIR—
Houseboats
on the
Jhelum

KASHMIR—
The Dal
Lake

KASHMIR—*Nanga Parbat* (26,620 *ft.*)

PART VI

EASTERN INDIA

Eastern India is a land of great rivers, the most celebrated of them being the holy Ganga. From its source near Gangotri in the snow-clad Himalayas to its mouth on the Bay of Bengal, every inch of this 1,500-mile long river is sacred to Hindus.

Towering over the Gangetic plain rise the awe-inspiring peaks of the Himalayas. One of the passes across these

CALCUTTA—An aerial view

forbidding mountains runs northwards from Darjeeling, the beautiful hill station of West Bengal, and serves as a highway for trade with Tibet.

Blessed with heavy rainfall and fed by great rivers the alluvial plains of Eastern India show mile after mile rice fields, interspersed with mango and bamboo groves and coconut palms. The tea plantations of Assam, and the jute fields of West Bengal feed that great centre of industry, Calcutta. Rich in coal, iron and mica, Eastern India is gradually becoming the "Rhineland" of India. Several multipurpose projects have been undertaken in this region and are expected to bring considerable economic benefits to the people. The best known of these is the Damodar Valley Project modelled on the Tennessee Valley Authority of the U.S.A.

BUDH GAYA

Seven miles from Gaya is the sacred Buddhist site of Budh Gaya, where under a *pipal* tree Gautama meditated and attained enlightenment. This place has since become a centre of pilgrimage. Asoka erected a temple near the tree, and when the stone floor of the present temple was removed, foundations of an older building, believed to be the remains of the Asoka temple, were found.

The present temple of Budh Gaya, completely restored in the eleventh century, has a tower rising to a height of 180 ft. in the form of a slender pyramid. Access to it is through an eastern gate supported by pillars. A part of the ancient stone railing surrounding it belongs to the second century B.C. The *Vajarasan* marking the spot where the Buddha sat is no longer there, the one now existing being of a later date. There is also a *pipal* tree, believed to be a descendant of the original Bodhi-tree.

PATNA

Patna, the capital of Bihar spreads eight miles along the river Ganga. In Bankipur, a western extension of the city, are Government House, the Secretariat and the Museum.

At one corner of the Bankipur maidan is a huge beehive-shaped structure, the Gola, 90 ft. high and 420 ft. at

111

BUDH GAYA

NALANDA—Ruins of the ancient university town

the base. It was built in the time of Warren Hastings for a granary and is one of the world's most interesting whispering galleries. From the top of the Gola is a panoramic view of the city and the river for miles around. The Khudabuksh Oriental Library, famous for its rare collection of Arabic and Persian manuscripts, possesses among others the only volumes saved from the sack of the Moorish University of Cordova. In the old city is the Har Mandir where Guru Gobind Singh, who made the Sikhs a militant community, was born.

The ancient city of Pataliputra lies buried under Patna. It was once the capital of Chandragupta Maurya, who defeated Alexander's General, Seleucus Nicator. It was also the capital of Asoka. Megasthenes came to Pataliputra as an Ambassador in the fourth century B.C. Excavations have unearthed interesting relics of the Mauryan age near the city of Patna.

NALANDA

Once a famous Buddhist university, Nalanda came into existence about the fifth century and was a great centre of learning for about 700 years. Hieun Tsang, the well-known Chinese traveller, who studied at the University in the seventh century, has left glowing accounts of its activities. It attracted students from all over India, South-East Asia and China.

The site has been excavated by the Archaeological Department of the Government of India. Visitors entering it from the eastern gate will see an array of monasteries on the east and a row of temples on the west. Nearby is a museum which has an interesting collection of antiquities recovered from the site.

JAMSHEDPUR

About 165 miles north-west of Calcutta, close to Bihar's rich iron and coal deposits, is India's picturesque "Steel Town," Jamshedpur. It was once a jungle-covered tract of land between two rivers. Owned by the Tata Iron and Steel Works, the gigantic steel works cover an area of 2½ sq. miles.

CALCUTTA

A mere village in the seventeenth century, Calcutta is today one of the biggest cities in the world. It is also one of the largest ports in the East, and the main outlet for the produce of West Bengal and the neighbouring States. It is the world's biggest centre for jute manufacture and has many paper and oil mills, iron foundries, tanneries and printing presses along the banks of the river Hooghly. Calcutta is the commercial metropolis of India.

In the centre of the city is a fine park known as the Maidan in which stands Fort William, the original British settlement. In the Maidan by the river Hooghly is the Victoria Memorial, Calcutta's finest building, which has many objects of interest associated with the long reign of Queen Victoria. East of the Maidan is Calcutta's main business centre, Chowringhee, a two-mile stretch of clubs, shops and hotels and to the north is Government House. At Alipore

CALCUTTA—The New Howrah Bridge

are Belvedere, once the country house of Warren Hastings, and the Zoological Gardens. Among the other places of interest are St. John's Church, Calcutta's oldest Christian place of worship (Job Charnock's mausoleum is in the grave-yard), the Kalighat temple, the Jain temple, the Belur Math, the headquarters of the Mission founded by Swami Vivekananda, and the temple of Dakshineswar where his *guru*, the famous saint Shri Ramakrishna Paramahansa, lived. The Botanical Gardens founded in 1786 contain a 170-year old banyan tree which is 1,000 ft. in circumference. It is said that its branches can shelter three regiments of soldiers. The New Howrah Bridge is a remarkable feat of engineering.

Calcutta has first-rate golf courses, a splendid race course, and a gay cold weather season.

SANTINIKETAN

A hundred miles from Howrah is Bolpur station. Once an insignificant village, it is now world famous, for two miles from it lies Santiniketan, " the abode of peace," where Rabindranath Tagore, the great poet of India, founded the Visva-Bharati University, a new experiment in education and a centre of Indian culture.

Fully co-educational and mainly residential, the university has faculties for the study of comparative religion, philosophy, Chinese and Indian classics, and the fine arts. It attracts students from all over India and beyond the seas.

Among the places worth seeing in Santiniketan is Rabindra Bhavan, where the poet's personal belongings, his manuscripts, his paintings and the various editions of his work are kept in a museum. The poet's mud-hut, where he wrote many of his famous books, is also an object of interest to the visitor.

DARJEELING

Darjeeling (7,000 ft.) is a beautiful hill station on a mountain ridge amid delightful forest scenery. From here one can see the Himalayas in all their majesty, range upon range of perpetual snow culminating in Kanchanjungha, 28,146 ft. high. Tiger Hill, seven miles from Darjeeling, gives an excellent view of Mount Everest.

SANTINIKETAN—Poet Tagore's university

SANTINIKETAN—Poet Tagore's residence

DARJEELING

Darjeeling (Rdo-rje-gling) means "the place of the *dorje*," the mystic thunderbolt of the religion of the Lamas. With its forest glades ablaze with rhododendrons, delightful walks, quaint nearby villages, interesting hill-folks—Lepchas, Bhutias, Tibetans and Nepalese—thronging its bazars, and its proximity to the forbidden land of Tibet, Darjeeling is a charming hill resort.

It is 369 miles by rail from Calcutta. At Siliguri the light mountain railway, a great engineering feat, begins its zigzag ascent to Darjeeling, 51 miles away.

SHILLONG

Well-planned and carefully laid out, Shillong, in the Khasi and Jaintia Hills, is the capital of Assam. It is surrounded by country different from that of the Himalayan resorts and not unlike the lowlands of Scotland. The city is 4,900 ft. above sea level and has pine woods, charming walks, golf links, a race course and good hotels. The temperature rarely exceeds 80 degrees F.

There is a good motor road from Shillong to Cherrapunji, which has the highest rainfall in the world. The record rainfall in the town in 1861 was 905 inches of which 365 inches fell in July alone.

IMPHAL

Imphal, the capital of Manipur, lies in a lovely valley and is of 2,600 ft. above sea level. There are several large lakes in Imphal which provide duck shooting in winter.

118

Imphal is specially well known for Manipur dances and handloom products.

BHUVANESWAR

Bhuvaneswar, the temple city, is the new capital of Orissa. Of its temples—once said to number 7,000—not more than 100 remain. They exhibit a variety of architectural styles. The finest are the great Lingaraj temple and the temples of Bhagavati, Parvati, Mukteswar, Ananta Vasudeva, Brahmeswar Bhaskareswar, and Parasurameswar.

On the hills known as Udayagiri and Khandagiri, a few miles from Bhuvaneswar, are caves, once occupied by Jain monks, containing remarkable carvings, the earliest of which date back to the second century B.C.

A bridegroom from the Naga tribe, Assam

PURI

Situated on the eastern sea coast, Puri, besides being a popular health and holiday resort, is a place of pilgrimage. In the centre of the town is the well-known shrine of Jagannath built in the thirteenth century, 192 ft. high, and crowned with Vishnu's wheel and flag. In front of the eastern gate of the temple is a marble pillar, an exquisite piece of carving. Maharaja Ranjit Singh of the Punjab, it is said, bequeathed the Kohinoor to the temple. His successor, however, failed to carry out the bequest.

During the Car Festival, held in June or July every year, the image of Jagannath is carried on a big car 45 ft. high and 25 ft. sq. supported on sixteen wheels, 7 ft. in diameter. The car is pulled by eager devotees.

KONARAK

Twenty miles north of Puri, along the coast, or about fifty miles by road is the Black Pagoda of Konarak, so called in contrast to the white temple of Puri. This famous pagoda, one of the marvels of India, was built by Narasingha Deva I, who ruled Orissa from 1238 to 1264, in honour of Surya, the Sun God. The monument must have been of colossal size, for the magnificent porch, the only portion of the ruined shrine now standing, is so immense as to form a landmark for miles around.

Exquisite carvings and monumental statuary characterize the Black Pagoda. Life-size lions and elephants, figures and thrones, scenes of battle and the chase, all carved with great imagination and skill, testify to the high standard of ancient Indian art, sculpture and engineering.

Of the Black Pagoda, Sir John Marshall writes: "There is no monument of Hinduism, I think, that is at once so stupendous and so perfectly proportioned."

BHUVANES-WAR—The Lingaraj temple

PURI—The Jagannath temple

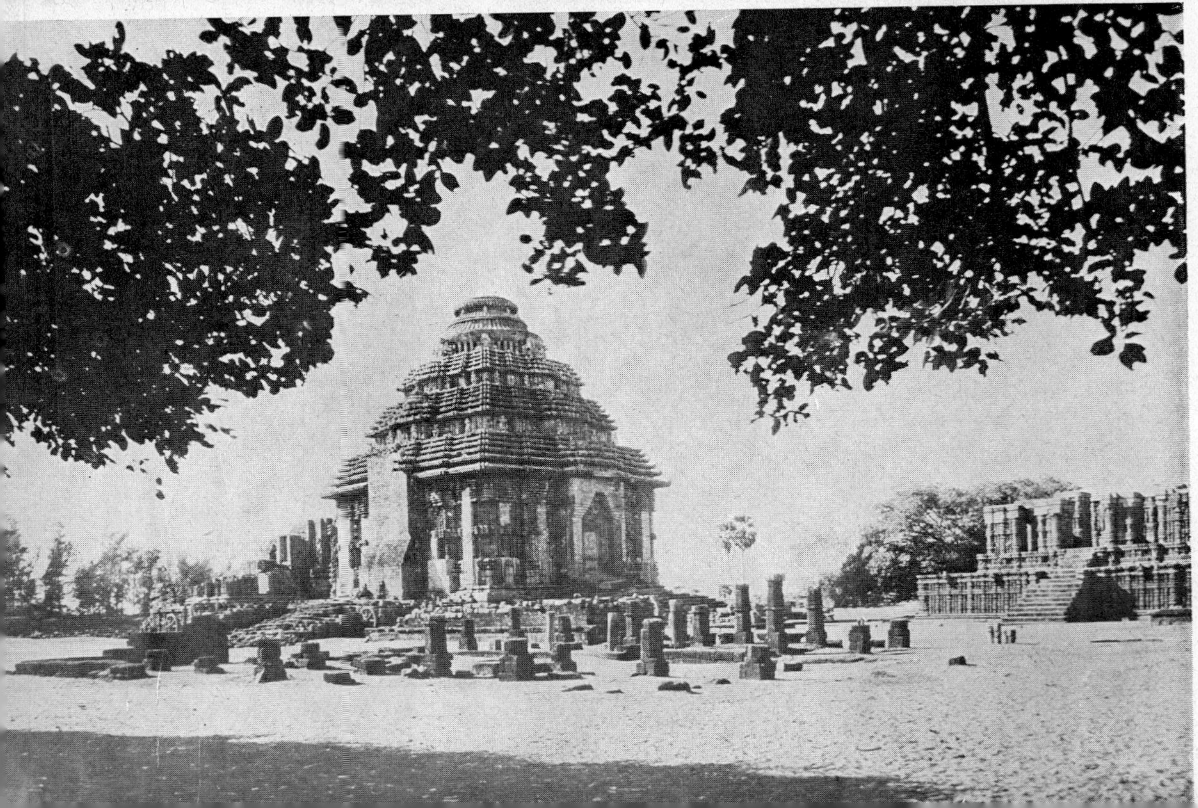

KONARAK —The Sun temple

Part VII

SOUTHERN INDIA

Southern India is essentially tropical, rich, fertile and densely populated. The Malabar coast has mountain scenery of great beauty, great waterways with peaceful lagoons and coconut palm-fringed shores. Further inland are Mysore with its pomp and pageantry on festive occasions, its exquisite handicrafts, its hills and jungles teeming with big game and the magnificent Jog Falls, and the Nilgiris, the lovely "Blue Mountains," with summer resorts at Ootacamund, Coonoor, and Kotagiri. Also included in Southern India are the fertile plains of the Coromandel coast. In the extreme south is Travancore-Cochin with a luxuriance of vegetation and wonderful scenery, unsurpassed in India.

Southern India is the seat of ancient Dravidian civilization, and its legacy of art and architecture is best expressed in its temples.

MADRAS

Madras is the third largest city of India. It is quite unlike India's other big towns, for it retains much of the spaciousness of the earlier days and many of its fine old houses. It spreads for about eight miles along the sea from the harbour and the business quarters in the north to the residential district of Adyar in the south. The Marina, a splendid esplanade by the sea, runs from Napier bridge to the Roman Catholic Cathedral at Old San Thome, founded by the Portuguese in 1504. Along the Marina there are several imposing public buildings.

In the Fort St. George founded in 1640 by Francis Day, Chief of the East India Company's factory at Armagon, is the oldest Protestant place of worship in India, St. Mary's Church.

MADRAS— The Marina

Madras city has several Hindu temples. Among the other places of interest in Madras are the 160 ft. high Light House from which the tourist can have a good view of the city, the Law College and the Museum. The Victoria Institute has specimens of south Indian handicrafts. Overlooking the sea amidst beautiful settings in Adyar is the headquarters of the Theosophical Society. The annual convention of the Society held here is attended by theosophists from all over the world.

MAHABALIPURAM—A temple by the sea

TIRUCHIRAPALLI—The Fort

An interesting excursion is to Mahabalipuram, or the
Seven Pagodas, as the Europeans have named it, thirty-
five miles from Madras. Here on the sea shore is a collection of ancient rock-hewn monuments which form some
of the most important architectural remains in Southern
India—monolithic temples, cave temples, monolithic figures
and carvings and sculptures, probably of the fifth or sixth
century A.D.

CONJEEVARAM

Conjeevaram, the "Golden City," forty-five miles south-west of Madras, has a long history. It was the capital of successive dynasties of Hindu rulers. Hieun Tsang, the Chinese traveller, who visited it in the seventeenth century A.D., has left an account of his sojourn there. Buddhism, Jainism and later Hinduism contended for supremacy in this ancient city for centuries.

TANJORE—The Great Temple

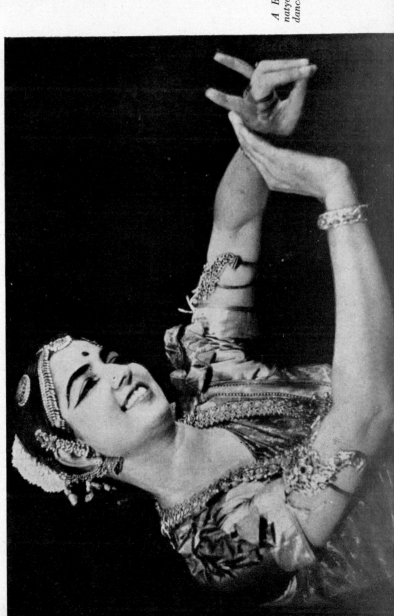

The city is remarkable for its temples and shrines. There is a Jain temple dating from the twelfth-thirteenth century. Even older are the two great temples of Vishnu and Siva built by the Pallava kings. The latter is noted for its lofty towers with fine porches, and a hall with 540 carved columns. In Little Conjeevaram, two miles away, is the Varadarajaswami temple which has a hall of beautifully carved pillars.

TIRUCHIRAPALLI (TRICHINOPOLY)

Tiruchirapalli is famous for its rock temple, said to have been built by the Pallavas.

SRIRANGAM

Two miles north of Tiruchirapalli, on an island formed by the bifurcation of the river Cauvery, is Srirangam, famed for its temple of Vishnu, the largest in Southern India. The temple contains a hall of a thousand columns and the sacred shrine of Ranganathaswami. The town is built round the temple in concentric squares.

A mile to the east of Srirangam is Jambukeswaram, a temple dedicated to Siva.

MADURAI (MADURA)

Madurai, popularly known as the "City of Festivals," was the capital of the Pandiyan kingdom which had an extensive sea-borne trade with Rome and Greece. The city became renowned in the seventeenth century under the Nayak kings, who contributed much to its architectural adornment.

The Great Temple, dedicated to the goddess Minakshi forms a parallelogram, 850 ft. by 750 ft., and is surrounded by nine gopurams (pyramidal towers), one of which is 150 ft. high. One of its principal structures is the Hall of a Thousand Pillars in which groups of figures are carved from single stones. These are marvels of industry, elaboration and exuberant imagination. The other important buildings in Madurai are all associated with the name of Tirumala Naik, the chief of which is his palace, the most perfect specimen of secular architecture in Madras State.

Madurai is also a textile centre, famous for hand-woven textiles and wood carving.

RAMESWARAM

The holy town of Rameswaram is built on an island in Palk Straits. It contains one of India's most venerated temples, perhaps the finest example of South Indian architecture. It is in the form of a quadrangular enclosure, 650 ft. by 1,000 ft. The temple is renowned for its vast pillared corridors nearly 4,000 ft. long.

MYSORE

A land of primeval forests, lovely cities, ornate shrines, and scenery abounding in all the charms of the tropics, Mysore makes a special appeal to tourists. Situated 2,000 to 3,000 ft. above sea level, its climate is mild and salubrious.

Mysore's history goes back to the days of Asoka, three of whose minor rock edicits are to be found in the extreme north of the State. Later it was the cradle of three great dynasties—the Kadambas, the Hoysalas and the kings of Vijayanagar. Under the impetus provided by the Hoysala kings in the eleventh, twelfth and thirteenth centuries, architecture and sculpture developed greatly and achieved perfection. The delicacy of carving and mastery of design are best represented in the shrines and temples. The temples at Somanathpur, Belur and Halebid bear witness to the marvellous powers of invention and skill of India's master-builders.

Mysore has some of the largest pioneer industrial undertakings in India, such as the Hindusthan Aircraft Factory at Bangalore, the Gold Mines of Kolar, the Iron and Steel Works at Bhadravati, and the Sandal Oil Factory at Mysore. The State is also one of the largest producers of silk and soap in India.

Bangalore, the capital of the State, is a city of imposing buildings and public gardens. Chamraj Sagar, the large artificial lake, supplies drinking water to the city. It is twenty-two miles by road and well worth a visit. Nandi, a summer resort, 4,851 ft. above sea level, is connected with Bangalore by a light railway and a motor road.

Thirty miles from Maddur station on the rail route from Bangalore to Mysore, where the Maharaja generally resides, the tourist can see the famous waterfalls of Sivasamudram (Siva's Ocean). Here the river Cauvery divides and becomes two streams, each descending about 200 ft. in a succession of picturesque rapids and cascades. The surrounding hills clothed in dense forest add to the beauty of the scene. There is a large electric generating station at Sivasamudram.

The city of Mysore is a " Garden City." It stands by a rocky hill named after the goddess Chamundi. Mysore has attractive wide roads and many imposing buildings. The palace of the Maharaja within the old Fort is admittedly one of the most beautiful buildings in India.

The best time to visit Mysore is during the Dusserah festivities which are celebrated with pomp and pageantry for ten days in the city. On the tenth day, the Maharaja goes in a procession through the principal streets seated in a golden howdah on an elephant. Headed by camels and accompanied by elephants, richly caparisoned horses, palanquins, silver coaches, and standard-bearers with silken banners, the spectacle is one of splendour and magnificence. After sunset a review is held on the Bannimantap Maidan amidst a blaze of light.

From Mysore it is convenient to visit Krishnaraj Sagar, Somnathpur, Srirangapatna (Seringapatam) and Melkote. Krishnaraj Sagar, only ten miles away, is a large reservoir with a water area of fifty square miles. Lovely terraced gardens have been laid out by the side of the dam with beautiful lawns and beds of flowers, fragrant shrubs and shady walks, cascades and fountains. The shrine at Somnathpur, a distance of thirty-three miles, is a marvel of grace and beauty. Srirangapatna, some eleven miles from Mysore, is on a small island in the river Cauvery and was a fortress in the days of Tipu Sultan. Melkote, twenty miles from Srirangapatna, is a place of pilgrimage for Hindus, the great philosopher Ramanuja having settled there in the eleventh century.

Sravanabelgola, Belur and Halebid are three other places of great interest. One can visit them from Hasan which is connected with Mysore by road and railway.

At Sravanabelgola, according to tradition, the great Emperor Chandragupta Maurya, having taken a vow of renunciation, spent his last days as an ascetic in a rocky cave on a small hill. On a larger hill is to be found the tallest known monolithic statue in the world, erected in 983 A.D. Carved out of one huge boulder, it represents a Jain saint, Gomateswara, and stands 60 ft. high.

The temple of Belur, built 900 years ago, is an exquisite specimen of Hoysala art. Fergusson, an authority on Indian architecture, says : "There are many buildings in India which are unsurpassed for delicacy of detail by any

MYSORE—Dusserah procession

in the world but the temple of Belur surpasses even these for freedom of handling and richness of fancy."

The monuments of Halebid rank among the masterpieces of Hindu art, chief among them are the Hoysaleswara and Kedareswara temples. Of the former which was never completed, Fergusson writes: "Had but this temple been completed, it is one of the buildings on which the advocate of Hindu architecture would desire to take his stand. Every convolution of every scroll is different. No two canopies are alike and every part exhibits a joyous exuberance of fancy scorning mechanical restraint. All that is wild in human faith, or warm in human feeling is found portrayed on its walls."

Proceeding by train from Hasan to Tarikere, it is only a short journey by bus to Gringeri, a place of pilgrimage

MYSORE—The Hoysaleswara temple, Halebid

on the banks of the river Tunga, where the great philosopher Shankara founded one of his principal *maths* (monasteries). From Tarikere there is a train for Talaguppa. The renowned Gersoppa (Jog) Falls, seven miles away, are reached by car or bus. Flowing over a rocky bed 250 yards wide, the river Sharavati reaches a tremendous chasm, and descends 830 ft. in four cascades—the Raja, the Roarer, the Rocket and the Rani—a scene of unrivalled grandeur. The force of the falling water generates electricity in the Mahatma Gandhi Hydro-electric Works.

Mysore offers the sportsman excellent mahseer fishing, and big game hunting, including tiger, panther, bison and bear. There are occasional Kaddah operations to capture wild elephants in the famous Heggaddavankote forest.

OOTACAMUND

Ootacamund is the leading hill station of South India. Situated in the heart of the Nilgiris, at a height of 7,500 ft., it lies on a plateau, and has the appearance of a vast park. To the north-west of "Ooty," are splendid downs reminiscent of Sussex, while to the west, south and south-west, lofty hills add to the grandeur of the scenery. Although eleven degrees from the Equator, its climate is similar to the summer in England. Coonoor and Kotagiri are also pleasant health resorts in the Nilgiris.

KODAIKANAL

Kodaikanal, another hill resort of great natural beauty in South India, is fifty miles by road from Kodaikanal railway station. About 7,000 ft. above sea level, it has a lake three miles in circumference skirted by a good motor road. Among the places of interest in this hill resort are three charming waterfalls within easy reach, Coaker's walk, a favourite promenade, and an observatory. There is an abundance of big and small game within a few miles of Kodaikanal.

TRAVANCORE-COCHIN—Snake boat race

TRAVANCORE-COCHIN

The most beautiful and fertile region in South India is Travancore-Cochin. With a winter climate that is not unduly warm, it has many charms to offer the traveller within its domains.

It has a varied scenery ranging from a countryside of lakes, creeks and canals in the Cochin-Kottayam district where palm-leaf-thatched houses nestle beneath dense growths of coconut palms and bananas, and traffic is water-borne, to open country between Trivandrum and Cape Comorin, the most southerly point in India, flanked by spurs of the Western Ghats, gaunt, bare and rocky.

The dominant feature of Travancore-Cochin is the luxuriance of its vegetation. And striking indeed is the contrast between the rich green of the trees and plants and the warm red of the earth while the fragrance of spice gardens reminds one of Ceylon. The State has a wonderful highland zone—the region of Periyar with mountains rising 5,000 to over 8,000 ft., valleys adown the boulder-strewn beds of which dash foaming torrents, low hills covered with the densest of virgin jungle where the trees are festooned with chains of creepers and brilliantly hued orchids, the home of great herds of wild elephants, bison, tiger, bear, black panther and wild boar.

Here the Travancore-Cochin Government have set up a game sanctuary by marking off an area of 1,000 acres of forest land skirting the Periyar lake. From a boat on the lake, the tourist can at times see wild animals on the banks quenching their thirst in the lake.

Trivandrum, "the holy city of Ananta," the capital of Travancore-Cochin State, some two miles from the sea, is a modern city. It has many fine buildings, picturesquely situated on small hills, beautiful parks and wide avenues. It is also a religious centre which attracts pilgrims from all over India. Special attractions to visitors are the Picture Gallery in the Museum and the Palace Picture Gallery within the Fort, containing a representative collection of Eastern paintings and other works of art.

About seven miles south of Trivandrum is Kovalam, a pleasant seaside resort with good bathing facilities. Thirty-three miles southwards is Padmanabhapuram, one of the ancient capitals of Travancore. In the old palace, there are mural paintings of a high order. Twenty miles south of Padmanabhapuram is Cape Comorin, the Land's End of India. The Cape is sacred to Hindus and a famous shrine is situated here.

To the north of Trivandrum is the ancient town of Quilon. Further north is the busy sea-port of Alleppey which can be reached by boat along delightful back-waters or by car. North of Alleppey along the coast is the important port of Cochin. Rubber, timber, pepper, coconuts, ivories and other products of Malabar and the Western Ghats are exported from Cochin.

Facing Cochin, across one of the many lovely lagoons of the Malabar Coast, is Ernakulam, the second important city of Travancore-Cochin.

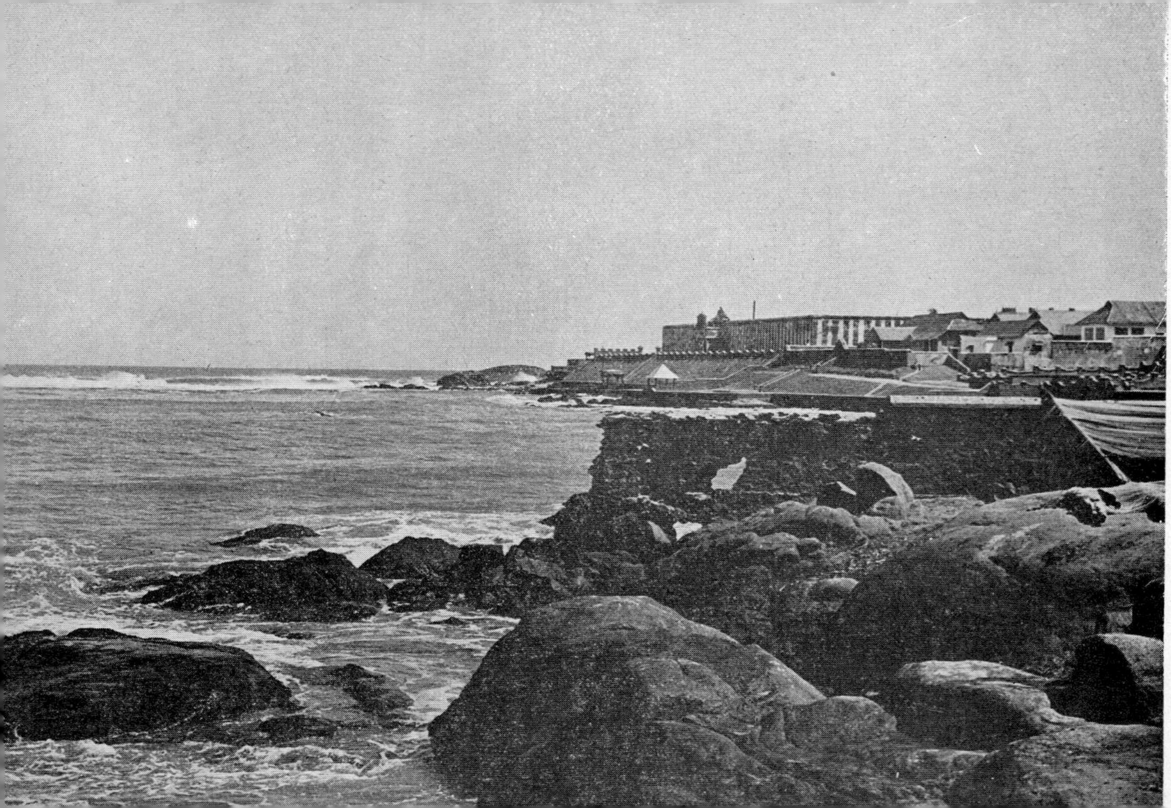

CAPE COMORIN

ACCOMMODATION

HOTELS

All principal cities have good Western style hotels. Charges for board and lodging in first-rate hotels at Bombay, Delhi, Calcutta and Madras vary from Rs. 25 to Rs. 40 per day. De Luxe suites are also available in certain hotels at Bombay, Delhi, Calcutta and Madras. Charges for these suites are from Rs. 70 to Rs. 100 per day.

In other places, the charges vary from Rs. 12 to Rs. 20 per day.

Since there is a heavy demand for hotel accommodation during the tourist season, intending visitors are advised to reserve accommodation well in advance preferably through tourist agencies. Normally two to four weeks' notice is required by important hotels during the tourist season. The hotel management makes special arrangements for foreign tourists. A hotel guide which gives the names of prominent Western-style hotels and their tariff is published by the Ministry of Transport and can be obtained from travel agencies, Indian Missions abroad and Regional Tourist Offices. State guest houses in the erstwhile princely States have also been opened for foreign tourists.

DAK BUNGALOWS AND REST HOUSES

Dak bungalows and rest houses are available at smaller centres. The keepers of dak bungalows will provide meals at short notice, but it is better to give intimation of the intended arrival in advance. The bed rooms in dak bungalows have adjoining baths and are provided with reasonably good furniture and light. There is a fixed fee for occupation and charges for meals supplied will be made. In service and comfort dak bungalows and rest houses cannot compare with large hotels. The former are convenient only for short stays. Special reservations for foreign tourists are made in dak bungalows and rest houses.

150

TRAVEL FACILITIES

AIRLINES

India is served by a network of airways. Most of the airlines use Dakotas and Vikings, the latter being used for non-stop flights between Bombay, Delhi and Calcutta. All airlines maintain an efficient staff consisting of well-qualified crew and other personnel. On every flight, there is an Air Hostess or a Steward to look after the passengers' comfort. There are lounges and restaurants at all the main airports and airlines provide free transport between the aerodrome and the town booking centre. Some of the airlines provide free meals and snacks during flights.

The normal free allowance of baggage per person is 44 lbs.

PROHIBITED ARTICLES

Government regulations do not permit the carriage of inflammable or explosive material in aircraft, and travellers are, therefore, reminded not to carry such things as cigarette lighters in their baggage or on their person. A full list of prohibited articles is displayed at the offices of the air companies.

FIRE ARMS AND AMMUNITION

Suitably packed fire arms and ammunition will be accepted on condition that they are declared and surrendered to the custody of the Commander of the aircraft before embarkation. Service personnel are permitted to retain their fire arms provided they are declared to the Commander of the aircraft before embarkation and are kept unloaded during the journey,

CANCELLATION OF RESERVATIONS

If the traveller has to cancel or defer his reservation, he should inform the Company at the earliest possible moment and return his ticket. No refund can be guaranteed, as this is governed by the circumstances of the cancellation and the rules in force.

AIR SERVICES

Name of Company	Route
1. AIR INDIA LTD., BOMBAY	*Bombay-Delhi (Night Service)* *Bombay-Karachi* *Bombay-Calcutta* *Bombay-Ahmadabad-Jaipur-Delhi* *Bombay-Madras-Tiruchirapalli- Colombo* *Bombay-Ahmadabad-Karachi* *Bombay-Madras* *Madras-Bangalore-Coimbatore- Cochin-Trivandrum*
2. AIR SERVICES OF INDIA LTD., BOMBAY	*Bombay-Keshod-Porbandar- Jamnagar-Bhuj* *Bombay-Jamnagar-Bhuj-Karachi* *Bombay-Bhavnagar-Rajkot* *Bombay-Poona-Bangalore* *Bombay-Indore-Gwalior-Delhi*
3. AIRWAYS (INDIA) LTD., CALCUTTA	*Calcutta-Bhuvaneswar-Visakha- patam-Madras-Bangalore* *Calcutta-Dacca* *Calcutta-Gauhati-Dibrugarh* *Calcutta-Baghdogra* *Calcutta-Nagpur-Bombay*
4. BHARAT AIRWAYS LTD., CALCUTTA	*Calcutta-Patna-Banaras-Lucknow- Delhi* *Calcutta-Allahabad-Kanpur-Delhi* *Calcutta-Chittagong* *Calcutta-Agartala-Gauhati-Tezpur- Jorhat-Mohanbari-Calcutta- Agartala-Silchar-Imphal*
5. DECCAN AIRWAYS LTD., HYDERABAD	*Madras-Hyderabad-Nagpur-Delhi* *Hyderabad-Bangalore* *Hyderabad-Bombay*
6. HIMALAYAN AVIATION LTD., CALCUTTA	*Night Service between Bombay, Delhi, Calcutta and Madras via Nagpur*

Name of Company	Route
7. INDIAN NATIONAL AIRWAYS LTD., NEW DELHI	*Delhi-Lahore* *Delhi-Calcutta* *Delhi-Jodhpur-Karachi* *Calcutta-Rangoon* *Delhi-Amritsar-Srinagar* *Srinagar-Jammu (shuttle service during April-December only)* *Delhi-Amritsar-Jammu-Srinagar* *Delhi-Srinagar (during April-July and September-November only)* *Calcutta-Patna-Katmandu*
8. KALINGA AIRLINES, CALCUTTA	*Calcutta-Agartala (Freight Service)*

RAILWAYS

Indian Railways have special arrangements for the convenience of tourists and the staff is instructed to provide all possible facilities to them. A separate time-table designed for the use of tourists is also published. Recognized travel agents undertake to make complete travel arrangements for tourists.

TOURIST COACHES

For those who wish to be independent of hotels, tourist coaches can be reserved which are very comfortable. In the coach the tourist can have his own personal servants and their continuous service, his private parlour and bedroom throughout the trip, and the meals he desires. He can dictate the menu in the same way as he does in his own home.

Coaches can be detached at any place the tourist wishes to visit, and remain there as long as he likes. They are fitted with electric fans and lights and bells. The new standard tourist coaches are supplied with refrigerators, crockery, cutlery, table linen, towels and bed linen.

153

SALOONS

Special four, six and eight wheeler saloons are also available on the broad gauge. Charges for these are as below :—

	4 wheeler			6 wheeler			8 wheeler		
	Rs.	A.	P.	Rs.	A.	P.	Rs.	A.	P.
Empty haulage ..	0	5	0	0	7	6	0	12	0 per mile
Haulage ..	1	0	0	1	6	0	1	12	0 ,,
Stoppage ..	16	0	0	20	0	0	25	0	0 per day

Accommodation in these saloons varies over the different railways. Generally, however, an eight-wheeler saloon provides accommodation for eight passengers and servants. The saloons have kitchens. They cost roughly 50 per cent more than First Class.

RESERVATION OF COMPARTMENTS AND BERTHS

Generally there are four berths in a First Class compartment and five in a Second Class compartment. There are also, on some railways, two-berth First and Second Class coupes. Each First and Second Class compartment and coupe, has its own lavatory, and many of these have needle spray or long baths as well. Berths can be reserved at the stations at which trains or carriages originate, on payment of a small fee. Berths can also be reserved at intermediate stations, on certain trains, provided 48 hours' notice is given, subject to accommodation being available.

LUGGAGE

The free allowance for luggage is :

First Class	..	..	60 seers or	123 lbs.
Second Class	..	..	40 seers or	82 lbs.
Inter Class	..	..	30 seers or	62 lbs.
Third Class	..	..	25 seers or	51 lbs.

FARES

The following are fares for each 50 miles :

Class	Rupees			Sterling			Dollar	
	Rs.	A.	P.	£	s.	d.	$	cents.
First ..	6	4	0	0	9	4½	1	31½
Second ..	3	11	0	0	5	5½	0	77
						Approx.		

First and Second Class passengers are provided with sleeping berths at night without extra charge. A passenger is allowed to break journey and halt one day for every 250 miles he travels.

RESTAURANT CARS

Dining cars are attached to most of the mail and express trains. Meals can also be obtained from restaurants or refreshment rooms at important stations. Western style food is served in restaurant cars as well as refreshment rooms.

AIR-CONDITIONED COACHES

Air-conditioned accommodation is available on the following routes:

Bombay (Central) to Amritsar *via* Delhi
Bombay (Victoria Terminus) to Howrah *via* Allahabad
Bombay (V.T.) to Madras (Central) *via* Poona and Raichur
Howrah to Delhi
Delhi to Kalka en route to Simla

The fare is 30 pies per mile. Berths in air-conditioned coaches may be reserved up to three months in advance of the journey.

IMPORTANT TRAINS AND THEIR ROUTES

(1) *Bombay-Calcutta Mail*

Two mail trains run between Bombay (V.T.) and Howrah each way, one *via* Nagpur and the other *via* Allahabad. On the latter route, air-conditioned accommodation is provided on trains leaving Bombay on Monday and Friday, and on trains leaving Howrah on Wednesday and Saturday. Dining car service is provided on these trains.

(2) *Frontier Mail*

This train which has air-conditioned accommodation runs every day between Bombay (Central) and Amritsar. Dining car service is provided.

(3) *Calcutta-Delhi-Kalka Mail*

This train runs daily between Howrah and Kalka *via* Delhi. Air-conditioned accommodation between Howrah

155

and Delhi is provided on trains leaving Howrah on Tuesday and Saturday, and Delhi on Monday and Thursday. Air-conditioned accommodation is also provided between Delhi and Kalka on Monday, Wednesday and Saturday in both directions. Dining car service is available on this train, except during night time.

(4) *Bombay Madras-Express*

This train runs between Bombay (V.T.) and Madras (Central) *via* Poona and Raichur. Dining car service is available. Limited air-conditioned accommodation is provided as shown below:

Date of each month	*Ex Bombay*	*Ex Madras*
1, 5, 9, 13, 17, 21, 25	2 coupe compartments	1 four-berth compartment
3, 7, 11, 15, 19, 23, 27	1 four-berth compartment	2 coupe compartments

ITINERARIES

Detailed itineraries may be obtained from any of the well-known travel agencies. Itineraries can be drawn up according to the port of entry into India, the length of stay and the means of transport to be used by the traveller. Glimpses of the charms of India may be had in a tour covering the following places, but the list is merely a selective one and not exhaustive.

Abu	Cape Comorin	Madras
Agra	Chitorgarh	Madurai
Ajanta	Cochin	Mysore
Allahabad	Darjeeling	Ootacamund
Amritsar	Delhi	Puri
Banaras	Ellora	Sarnath
Bangalore	Hyderabad	Santiniketan
Bhuvaneswar	Jaipur	Shillong
Bombay	Kashmir	Tiruchirapalli
Budh Gaya	Konarak	Trivandrum
Calcutta	Lucknow	Udaipur

SPORTS

Because of its well-defined seasons, India is able to provide more facilities for sports than many other countries, and visitors will find their particular requirements fully met. Racing, polo, golf, hunting, shooting, pig-sticking, fishing, yachting, winter sport, tennis, cricket, hockey and football offer entertainment and relaxation in their respective seasons in centres widely apart and at a comparatively low cost.

Tennis—Tennis is controlled by the All India Lawn Tennis Association through its affiliated State organizations. The standard of the game has considerably improved and India now participates in international tournaments. A new chapter in the history of Indian tennis was written when the first Asian Lawn Tennis Championship was held at Calcutta in December 1949 and India won the singles championship.

Hockey—Hockey may be regarded as the national game. Its standard is very high and India has won the Olympic Hockey Championship three times in succession. The game is controlled by the All India Hockey Federation. The Inter-State Championship trophy is a quaintly carved shield presented by the Maoris to the Indian team which toured New Zealand in 1938. The principal hockey tournaments are the Aga Khan Cup at Bombay and the Beighton Cup at Calcutta.

Cricket—Indian cricket has reached international standard and representative Indian teams have toured Commonwealth countries. It is controlled by the Board of Control for Cricket in India. There are 17 State Associations and they compete annually for the Ranji Trophy—the gold cup in memory of the famous Indian cricketer Prince "Ranji." Bombay is the headquarters of the Cricket Club of India and the Brabourne Stadium attached to it is one of the finest of its kind.

Football—Calcutta is the main centre of the game, although it is played in most cities in India. The game is

*A polo match
—Jaipur vs.
Argentine*

popular and provides excitement which equals that of an English cup tie. The principal competitions are the I.F.A. Shield at Calcutta, the Rover's Cup at Bombay and the Durand Cup at Delhi.

Polo—Polo is confined largely to the Army and Rajasthan, and India has produced some of the world's best polo players.

Golf—Golf is played in the chief cities of India and some of the golf courses in the country compare favourably with those in Europe. The casual visitor may have a game on payment of the usual green fee by arrangement with the local Secretary. Calcutta, Bombay, Delhi, Ootacamund and Gulmarg in Kashmir are the main golf centres. Annual competitions are held by all leading clubs.

Racing—Racing thrives in the principal cities of India. The standard of racing is high and the courses at Calcutta and Bombay compare with the best in the world, especially in the provision of comfort for race-goers. The chief events are the Indian Derby and the Eclipse Stakes of India, both run in Bombay, and the King's Cup at Calcutta.

Fishing—India offers unlimited and unrestricted opportunities of sport to the angler inasmuch as its rivers and lakes are abundantly stocked with a large variety of indigenous sporting fish, and fishing, with a few exceptions, is free to everyone and open all the year round. Furthermore, should the angler be fastidious and wish to go in for what was his favourite pastime at home among the trout, he will find opportunities in many of the hill stations where the European trout has been successfully introduced and a day's good sport can be had under ideal conditions.

Good deep sea fishing is available along the Travancore and Malabar coasts. The mahseer or Indian salmon is found in most of the large rivers of India, and as fighter it has few equals. The trout is found in hill streams, particularly in Kashmir, the Kulu Valley and Ootacamund.

Pig Sticking—Pig sticking or hunting the wild boar with a spear from horse back, is an exhilarating sport, for there are few animals in the world bolder than the wild boar. The chief centres for pig sticking are Meerut, Delhi, Mathura, Kanpur, Calcutta and Rajasthan.

Winter Sports—Winter sports are still in their infancy in India. One can, however, skate in hill resorts and ski at Gulmarg in Kashmir.

Other Games—The other sports include athletics, swimming, diving and yachting. Wrestling is very popular and big events are held annually in all big cities. Billiards is played in practically all important clubs, while table tennis and badminton have made rapid progress in recent years.

Flying Clubs—There are active flying clubs in most of the State capitals.

SHIKAR

Big Game—India has a large variety of wild animals, a number of which may be considered "Big Game" from the point of view of a sportsman with a rifle, and for the increasing number of those who hunt with a camera there are, besides these, smaller animals such as reptiles and countless birds which furnish an inexhaustible supply of subjects for photography.

Among the game animals there are species which afford as fine trophies as can be had in any other land.

India's net-work of 34,000 miles of railway and efficient motor transport make access to shooting grounds fairly easy. There are few shooting grounds more than a day's journey from the railway. Exception has, of course, to be made in regard to some parts of the Himalayas. The spring months are the best for big game shooting.

As regards the species which the sportsman can aspire to obtain, of the cat tribe there are three—the tiger, the panther and the cheetah. The lion is now found only in Saurashtra and is strictly protected. Of the bear there are four kinds; deer seven; antelope and gazelle six; goat eight; sheep three; and of the ox three. In addition there is the buffalo, the elephant and the rhinoceros. Then there are such rare animals as the Sikkim stag, the clouded leopard, the musk deer and the moose deer.

THE HIMALAYAS

In quest of markhor, the grandest of wild goats, and ibex the sportsman will wander among the magnificent mountain ranges of the higher Himalayas, while for wild yak, ovis ammon (the largest wild sheep), ovis vignei (shapu), ovis pseudois nahoor (bharal), Tibetan antelope and gazelle, he will visit the uplands of Ladakh, in Kashmir.

KASHMIR

In the lovely Kashmir valley he will find serow, black bear, and the famed Kashmir stag. Should he be more fortunate than most he may acquire the much coveted trophy of a snow leopard either in Ladakh, Lahoul, Spiti, or some other part of the snowy ranges where he may be hunting. At the Gate of Kashmir he may seek the fine markhor of the Kaj-i-Nag Mountains.

KISHTWAR TO KUMAUN

In the neighbouring country of Kishtwar the nimble goral will afford sport together with good climbing amid grand scenery, while life and limb may be risked (but one never hears of a fatality) in pursuit of tahr. Both these wild goats, as also bharal and black bear are found all the way to the east as far as eastern Kumaun, but there are no ibex or markhor east of the river Sutlej. The barking deer is available in most parts of the lower ranges while the panther is ubiquitous. One may adventure through Kumaun and beyond the Inner Line to the Tibetan border in search of yak and ammon.

THE TARAI

Less strenuous work awaits the sportsman in the tiger-haunted forest tract which marches for a thousand miles with the foothills of the Himalayas and is penetrated by a number of branch feeder lines. Most of these junctions are on the borders of, or in the forests where there are wild elephant (not to be shot), tiger, panther, sloth bear, sambar, spotted deer, swamp deer, hog deer, barking deer, four-horned antelope and also nilgai.

K

Wild elephants

Capture of wild elephants

THE PUNJAB

Black buck (antelope) and ravine deer (gazelle) are at their best in the plains of the Punjab.

ASSAM

In this State are elephants (proscribed rogues may be shot) and buffaloes besides the species listed for the sub-Himalayan tract. Nilgai is not found in Assam and swamp deer may be shot in some parts only. The great Indian rhinoceros is still met with in Assam and in the Nepal Tarai but is fully protected everywhere to prevent extinction. The bison is found in Assam, and the takin, which has been obtained by but few sportsmen, can be sought in the Mishmi Hills.

BENGAL, BIHAR AND ORISSA

In the reserved forests of these States tiger and other game animals can be hunted. In the Sunderban jungles south of Calcutta there are man-eaters, and substantial rewards are offered for their destruction. Rhinoceros, once common, is no longer found in this area. There is plenty of crocodile shooting in the river Mahanadi.

CENTRAL INDIA AND RAJASTHAN

Rulers of the erstwhile princely States took just pride in tigers and other game animals preserved in their forests. Most of these forest blocks are now open to shikaris. The record sambar for all India was shot in Bhopal. In Saurashtra are to be found the only wild lions in Asia. They are strictly preserved.

MADHYA PRADESH

With the exception of hog deer, which is not found south of the Uttar Pradesh Tarai, all the game animals of that tract inhabit the jungles of Madhya Pradesh which is perhaps the most sought-after tiger-hunting ground in India. The sambar of the Madhya Pradesh forests carry the finest horns of that species in India, though grand heads can be met with in many other parts of the country also. Swamp deer may be shot but in one locality only.

A tiger on a kill

Crocodiles

A tiger shoot

Bisons are to be found in fair numbers in the eastern parts and in some other forest divisions, while a few buffaloes are left in a portion of the country adjoining the erstwhile Bastar State, as well as in Jeypur and the area bordering the Mahanadi river.

BOMBAY STATE

The extensive northern and central forests of Bombay State are now nearly denuded of game animals for which they were once famous. The forests of the Belgaum circle are, however, well-stocked and contain elephant, tiger, bison, panther, beer, and deer in plenty.

SOUTH INDIA, HYDERABAD, MYSORE, AND TRAVANCORE-COCHIN

Hyderabad State, once well known for tiger shooting, still provides good sport. In Mysore State there are elephant, bison, and other game animals, while tigers are classed as " game."

Bisons are fairly plentiful all along the Western Ghats, and in the outlying forest division from Belgaum to the South of Travancore, also in the Eastern Ghats. Elephants are numerous in Orissa and in fair numbers in all the jungles of the Western Ghats, and in north Coimbatore. In the Nilgiri hills and the hills of Travancore-Cochin is the fine wild goat called the 'Nilgiri Ibex,' an animal akin to the tahr of the Himalayas.

From the above survey it can be realized that the energetic sportsman visiting India for big game hunting has before him a great number of localities from which to select his shooting grounds, and some of the most interesting and distinctive game animals in the world to win him the trophies he desires.

The Government have recognized a few experts for organizing big game hunting trips in various parts of the country. Their names are available with travel agents and the Government's Regional Tourist Offices. They make all necessary arrangements including the hiring of weapons.

Detailed information in respect of big game hunting is contained in the publication entitled " Big Game

Hunting in India and the Game Animals of India." This is a priced publication and can be obtained from the Manager of Publications, Old Secretariat, Delhi.

Small Game—During the winter months small game is plentiful and many an enjoyable day can be spent even near the big cities. Near Delhi one can shoot duck, goose, snipe and partridge, grey and black. The black partridge frequents the sugarcane patches and to flush the bird a rope is rustled across cane tops. Within a few hours of Calcutta very good duck and snipe shooting is to be found and there are many local shikaris willing to take visitors out. Special facilities for duck shooting exist in the Chilka lake area in Orissa.

The rice fields in West Bengal are full of snipe in winter, and there are numerous lakes in the Gangetic valley, which are the winter haunt of the wild duck. The sandy desert areas of Rajasthan are the home of the sand-grouse. There are several varieties, the one most prized is the imperial sand-grouse.

In all forest areas the jungle fowl are plentiful and these birds provide splendid shooting as they flit in and out.

The pheasant, the kalij, the koklass, the chir, the moonal and the crimson tragapan live on the higher slopes of the Himalayas. These birds are most difficult to shoot.

The chikor, a hill partridge, is prized by sportsmen and is found in Kashmir.

The bustard, the florican, the quail, the green pigeon and several other varieties of wild pigeon swell the list of small game in India.

EQUIPMENT

Tourists contemplating big game shooting are advised to provide themselves with rifles of suitable calibre, together with licences for their import into India as well as police licences for their retention. It is also necessary to obtain permits to shoot in the areas selected besides arranging for accommodation and transport, such as the hiring of lorries, bullock carts, boats and porters. In all the principal cities there are large stores where guns, ammunition and fishing tackle can be obtained.

PROHIBITED BORES

Certain bores (such as those used by the Army and the Police) namely, .303, .450 in the case of rifles and .38, .441 and .455 in the case of pistols and revolvers are strictly prohibited to the visitor.

It is important that all fire-arms are produced before the Customs Inspector and full details of these entered in the space provided on the back of the Customs form. All fire-arms and ammunition, excepting service pattern revolvers forming part of a military officer's equipment, are liable to duty. If re-exported within 2 years, seven-eighth of the duty paid is refunded, provided the prescribed procedure is followed for claiming such refunds. Arms which are not covered by licence will be taken to the Customs House from where they will be cleared on production of the necessary licence and on payment of duty. It is possible for a passenger who does not wish to clear his weapons to leave them in the custody of the Customs' authorities. They will be put on board the steamer by which he leaves India on payment of rent and delivery charges. Any travel agent will undertake these formalities for the visitor.

(For the Himalayas)

A suitable weapon is a .375 Magnum magazine. The .318 Accelerated Express is also good for the hills. There are other small bore rifles, the choice is with the individual.

(For the Plains)

For tiger, buffalo, bison, elephant, a D. D. II. V. rifle of .470 or approximate calibre is suitable. Some prefer .450 or .400. Physique may determine the choice. Whatever the bore, the rifle must be fitted with non-automatic safety catch, safe and noiseless sling swivels and noiseless webbing sling.

A shot gun is a useful weapon for following up wounded carnivora and for bird shooting.

173

174

176

ɔʀ 𝔉𝔲𝔩𝔩 30 CENTURIES

till the rise and growth of the modern European Powers, India remained the proud mistress of the Eastern seas. Her extensive coastline and strategic position helped her maintain her naval supremacy for so long. Indian merchants travelled far and wide, cultivating trade relations with the whole of the then known world extending from Japan to Rome.

We feel proud of these glorious traditions of India and consider it a sacred duty to reinstate our Motherland in the forefront of the seafaring countries.

INDIA STEAMSHIP CO., LTD.

Regular Cargo Service between
INDIA –U. K.–CONTINENT and
around the coast of India & Ceylon

Managing Agents : LIONEL EDWARDS LIMITED.

D-1, CLIVE BUILDINGS, CALCUTTA.

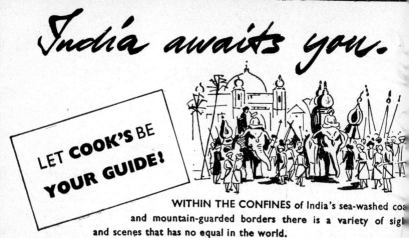

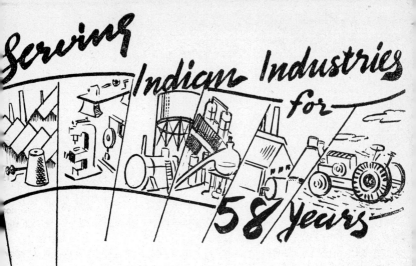

INDEX TO ADVERTISERS